Changing the Journey's Challenges into Opportunities

TAKES MORE THAN HEART

Dennis Mellen

 FriesenPress

Suite 300 - 990 Fort St
Victoria, BC, V8V 3K2
Canada

www.friesenpress.com

ISBN
978-1-5255-9182-2 (Hardcover)
978-1-5255-9181-5 (Paperback)
978-1-5255-9183-9 (eBook)

1. Biography & Autobiography, Personal Memoirs

Distributed to the trade by The Ingram Book Company

DEDICATION

This book is dedicated to all first responders and in particular to the EMTs, firefighters in the Carnation, Washington, and Fall City, Washington, fire stations, and the emergency room staff at Overlake Hospital in Bellevue, Washington. Your commitment, resolve, grit, and persistence in maintaining your rescue skills and applying those medical skills is instrumental in saving lives. Yes, the guy you saved twelve years ago from the "It's A Bitch" bike trail in Tolt-McDonald Park is still kicking, thanks to you.

I owe gratitude to my best friends, Tom and Carma Kemp, who encouraged me to write my book, and Ken Adams. I would also like to include my wife, Heidi, my bulkhead against the storm and my North Star and my four fine sons whom I admire for not only their talent but their caring and integrity.

You all make a difference.

TABLE OF CONTENTS

ACKNOWLEDGMENTS

I want acknowledge all the donors who helped me with promoting this book especially: Chrissy Palffy, Connie Policar, Ron Tranquilli, Betty Mellen, Jud Wells, Nick Daffern, Mary and Ray Fitzgerald, Fran Fulghum, Beverly Gabriel, Joan Gier, Kitty Hoeck, Ken Adams, Ed Laine, Mike Mellen, Dave Lawrence, Brent Hall, Jim Freeman, Carma and Tom Kemp and Roger Bailey. Without your assistance readers would never discover this book.

The baseball coaches who have patiently taught, cajoled and guided me in my coaching development, thanks for mentoring me especially Coach Murrdog, Coach Mike, Coach Pec, Coach Belo, Coach Sank, and my Baseball Sensei. You guys are rock stars and always make my learning curve look vertical. I am still learning from you.

PROLOGUE

Have you ever wondered if you truly have grit and perseverance? Do you look at challenges as obstacles or as opportunities to learn? Can people teach themselves to be comfortable in uncomfortable situations? Do you know anyone who has never faced adversity? Do you believe in second chances?

Publishing a personal book can be intimidating and not because of the process. Well yeah, the process is intimidating, too. Once published—if you get that far—everyone knows "your business." I mean, you will be forever branded as the cancer guy, the guy who landed a plane in the river, the heart-attack guy, or the whatever-the-adversity-was-you-faced guy. People may doubt you, or critics might say you are perpetuating victimhood or looking for sympathy. I always admire the writers who reveal their personal vulnerability so you can learn from their experience. Rather than hunkering down in shame within their self-protection biodomes, these writers expose a chink in their public images, and they hope you can relate. They usually write something personal, try to make a difference, and involve some sort of "career" or "life do-over."

My book is different, because it deals not only with a heart-attack recovery but also the career do-over aspect. Most books on heart attacks deal with the medical events and the physical recovery. But what about the devastating effects of never working at your life's work, your chosen career, again? My book also applies the lessons learned to everyday adversity and mental-performance aspects of leadership. What guides your business and athletic mind?

The intent of this book is to illustrate the value of the constant, relentless pursuit of "what's important next" when dealing with adversity, learning from your errors, establishing and maintaining your relationships, and persevering. "What's important next" means to stop dealing with the past and deal with the next event—your next reaction to influence the outcome. In no way is my intent to trivialize anyone who has ever suffered a serious setback. This book is my story of my life-changing event. My story is not without self-doubt and self-pity. This is a story about staying positive, or in some cases, in resolving yourself to stay positive, and in no way represents me as a Pollyanna. To paraphrase famed football coach Vince Lombardi, never stop pursuing the perfect version of yourself, knowing that you may never obtain it, but that in the pursuit, you may obtain the best version of yourself.

Although I led teams, departments, and organizations, I am not a Ph.D., nor have I done extensive studies on leadership behavior. My biography includes:

- Twenty-eight-year Alaska Airline captain and fleet captain of five hundred and fifty pilots and forty instructors, retired
- Twenty-year Air Force LtCol chief pilot and command pilot, retired
- Directing and leading large training programs
- Directing and leading flight standards
- Consulting, teaching, and coaching, including leading/directing operational teams
- Certified International Air Transport Association flight safety auditor
- Worldwide instructing and teaching in such places as Kenya, the Philippines, and Cape Verde

I do have a certification in athletic mental performance, which blends well with business and leadership. You will see references to many highly qualified individuals who lead the way in their areas of expertise. I respectfully use these individuals to re-enforce the concepts presented as they continue to inspire me.

It took four years of struggling to find a new career, and my purpose. Initially, I cast my net searching for jobs similar to flying for a major airline. I tried to recapture my old feeling: *This ain't work. I love this.* I failed, because there was no equivalent airline for me, much less a job similar to airline captain, and so, the disappointment of never flying again hung ominously over my head—a crushing reminder of how one event can change your whole world.

How do I set my story up? Let me take you back to a Seattle "Bluebird Day." That's what they call those clear, blue-sky days with nary a cloud. A "Bluebird Day" is stunning. I mean, you can actually see Mount Rainier! Seattle has two weather indicators: If you cannot see Mt. Rainier, it's raining; if you *can* see Mt. Rainier, it's going to rain. But these "Bluebird Days" are truly incredible, and great for long bike rides in the Cascade foothills. So, on October 14, 2008, a fifty-six-year-old airline pilot with a day off decides, "Today is a good day to tackle 'It's A Bitch'." This single-path bike trail is known in the vernacular of the area as IAB. The day portends ominously.

1 – HEART-STOPPING MOMENT

"Nobody has ever measured, not even poets,
how much the heart can hold."
—Zelda Fitzgerald

Starting near the confluence of the Tolt and Snoqualmie Rivers, IAB begins at Tolt-MacDonald Park. Not wanting to park on the east side of the river and have to cross the narrow suspension footbridge, I park on the west side, just off Tolt Hill Road and approximately one-half mile from the start of IAB.

The trail description reads, "The first trail to the larger trail system is called IAB (It's A Bitch). IAB does live up to its name as you bike/hike 1 mile and gain 500ft, but once at the top there are no more big climbs. The trails are all rolling fun, technical. There are a few great views of the Snoqualmie Valley from up top at Tolt, but most of the trails are classic western Washington lowland forests—ferns, cedar, fir, roots, etc."

"The Iron Man" portion seems to be that first mile; however, I tell myself, there is no way I am swimming in the mountain-stream-fed Snoqualmie River and running a marathon after this bike ride to complete the three Iron Man events. Today is just a fun bike ride.

(Do you know Dr. James Gillis? He has competed in six double "Iron Man" triathlons. That is, you compete in a triathlon one day, and twenty-four hours later, follow it with another, and he did this at the age of fifty-nine! That won't be me today, tomorrow, or ever. I just wanted a good workout ride, and IAB looked like an opportunity on this "Bluebird Day.")

Decked out in fairly conservative black-with-blue-striped bike shorts, a black dry-fit shirt, black helmet, and gray bike shoes, I'm not one of those bikers festooned as Nino Baldacci from the Italian bike racing team. (Have you seen some of those bike outfits people wear? I mean, come on! Mardi Gras outfits are more conservative. But really, unless you are actually in the bike portion of an Iron Man, which is about 112 miles traversed in a little over four hours' time, who are you impressing?)

The temperature is a comfortable 61° with a light breeze. No worries about hypothermia or heat exhaustion. My car's parked; I unlock my bike from the rack and recheck the tire inflation for the fourth or fifth time. (You can't take the pre-flight out of the pilot; you know what I mean?) I follow the dirt road paralleling the Snoqualmie River, avoiding one huge puddle, but by necessity, riding right through the next puddle with the back tire gently flipping a muddy spray up my back. The anticipation builds for a great day of biking the Tolt-MacDonald trail complex.

Reaching the trailhead, I pass some of the King County Park System yurts used for camping. (Yurts? Is that shorthand for yogurt shake? What the heck is a Yurt? Yurt: a circular tent of felt or skins on a collapsible framework, used by nomads in Mongolia, Siberia, and Turkey.) These particular ones are made with lumber and canvas, semi-permanently spaced about one hundred yards apart. *Wow, will I need to outride a Mongol horde?* I make a reference for a future camping trip possibility, even though my wife's idea of camping is a three-star hotel. Maybe my sons might be interested.

The initial climb isn't too steep, but it is uphill. The yurt area is clear, and the foliage neatly trimmed back, but the beginning point of IAB is not readily apparent. And signage? Well, signage would spoil the pristine, natural look. After a couple fruitless sallies into dead-ends behind several yurts, through fits and starts, I spy the trail leading off to the north with a long steady climb under some very tall, verdant ferns and 150-foot Douglas firs. (I think the last time I used the word "verdant" was studying for the S.A.T.s, but I digress.)

I pedal in a somewhat-low gear, making steady progress uphill at about five mph, according to my handy-dandy speedometer when I read it at the first switchback. Turning left, the trail steepens considerably, but I'm still riding fairly fast for the incline: a screaming three mph. The forest canopy is thick, blocking a lot of the sunlight, with bright yellow shafts of light streaming through intermittently. The trail is wet and filled with pine needles, looking like a scene from *Star Wars,* and any minute, I'm expecting a speeder to come by with a stormtrooper, or even Luke Skywalker, at the wheel.

On the next switchback, the incline changes dramatically, and I am forced to the lowest gear. My speed drops to that of a circus performer riding a unicycle. I can feel my lungs burn, but I'm loving it because of the challenge. To jump off the bike and walk … well, that's for wieners. Still, I wonder why this bravado is necessary. I mean, I'm not in Mardi Gras colors. Workouts don't need to be maximum efforts, and Nino Baldacci is nowhere around. What's wrong with a nice, easy workout anyway? I've been on many three- to five-hour bike rides without pushing myself to the max. *Not today! I will not lose to the Italian biking team.*

Themes from my college days, from basic training and "Doolie Year" and beyond at the Air Force Academy, echo in my mind: *Don't let your classmates down! Stick together! Better your obstacle course time! Compete!* And then there's the ultimate: Don't be a wussy (or something similar). Thinking back, running in a group allowed me to continue in the longer runs because of the encouragement from the other cadets. We ran in flights of thirty doolies or so, singing and chanting all the usual "joadies." The "joadies," or military cadence songs, helped us get in that mindless zone where time passes so very quickly and the exercise pain seemed to evaporate. We are better as a team than we ever are as one.

Today, I'm determined to make it non-stop to the top of IAB as the steepness lessens for about a quarter of a mile, leading westward away from the edge of the hill. *A drink of water would be nice,* I think. *Maybe at the top.* I hit another switchback, and the trail, while still steep, is not nearly as steep as before, so I shift into a higher gear and push my speed up considerably. I spy a log across the trail ahead and use the bicycle's shock absorbers to expertly log-hop over it without getting off the bike. My thought process tells me that I'm doing the same amount of work as before but moving faster in the higher gear. But who am I racing? There's nobody else on the trail. They are all working today, and I am a lucky, healthy, FAA Class I physical specimen.

Besides, chicks dig me, right? I know. This comment comes from a "knuckle dragging Neanderthal throwback." (Astronaut Mike Mullane, in his book *Riding Rockets,* said that his being non-PC was a result of graduating from West Point or "the socially retarded" school. Of course, being an Air Force Academy grad, I am only slightly more sophisticated, but with a subtle pinch of irreverence.)

I round a curve near the top, and I'm working myself very hard. My breath comes in controlled gasps and then uncontrollable huffs, but I'm almost to the top. No time to let up now—only a less manly man would do that. I feel the sweat sweeping down my back, bringing waves of wetness. Sweat is dripping from my eyebrows, from my wrists. My gloves are soaked. I can see a clearing ahead and blue sky above me. Maybe I should take a water break. Maybe I should sit down and look across the valley to the river below. After all, the trail description says it's only a mile, and a 500-foot elevation climb, and I'm almost there anyway. Nobody will know I rested.

I stop, swing my leg over the rear wheel, and take a couple of steps. Man, I need to sit down. Finding a log, I let my bike fall over, and I settle on a mossy black tree trunk, cradling my chin in my hands, my elbows on my knees. *Man, I don't feel so good.* I close my eyes for what seems a minute and then hear the voices of two men asking if I'm okay. I weakly answer in the affirmative, and that I just need to rest for a minute. For some reason, I have an urge to lay down. The voices are saying something unintelligible. I roll to my knees and promptly projectile vomit the contents of my stomach and quite possibly pass out. I don't know. I don't know what's happening.... I don't know....

2 – FACED DEATH AND WINKED

"Sometimes it's okay if the only thing
you did today was breathe."
—Yumi Sakugowa

Slowly, I awaken from what feels like an early morning, wine-induced stupor, kind of not sure where I am. The lights in the room feel like the spotlights used in an interrogation. *"We have ways of making you talk, and they are not pleasant."* I can't quite open my eyes, but feel something attached to my hand. Is that an electrical lead? Am I being tortured for information? My eyes come into focus, and my brother, Matt, is hovering over me. I look at him and say, "Hey, butthead." He laughs, reaches over, and hugs me with tiny tears at the corners of his eyes.

"Dennis, you had us scared."

My mind races, and somehow, I know I had an emergency and am in a hospital bed. Some of the other family members walk in, all smiling, and start filling me in on the last three days. While I was semi-conscious up on IAB, the two hikers had basically saved my life. One remained with me while the other ran down the hill, dialing 9-1-1 for help, because the cell-phone reception is poor on IAB. I guess the "Can you hear me now" guy has not made it to IAB yet. I am completely stunned when it is revealed that I'd had a heart attack! A myocardial infarction, to be more precise, which is "the interruption of blood flow to a part of the heart, causing damage to the heart muscle. The most common symptom is chest pain or discomfort, which may travel into the shoulder, arm, back, neck, or jaw. Often it occurs in the center or left side of the chest and lasts for more than a few minutes. The discomfort may occasionally feel like heartburn (check). Other symptoms may include shortness of breath (check), nausea (vomiting, check), feeling faint (check), a cold sweat or feeling tired (check and check)." And for added drama, death is a pretty recognizable symptom as well, although not treatable. *Wait, what? Not Disco Denny! I mean, I work out three to four times a week!*

The mind has a strange, protective strategy for dealing with traumatic events. My wife, Heidi, began tying together the details for me, everything since I had passed out on the trail, all of which seemed vaguely familiar yet blocked from memory. As I laid on the trail in apparently excruciating pain, one of the rescue hikers had dialed my wife and relayed our conversation, which—as she relates the details—involved chest pains and Doctor Denny's assessment, "Heidi, I think I'm having a heart attack."

While still on the phone with the man, Heidi immediately left her outpatient-medical-facility job, racing by car to the Tolt-MacDonald Trail complex, some half hour away, not actually knowing where it was located. In retrospect, she remembers nothing about the actual route she took but firmly believes divine intervention guided her to where my car and the unnoccupied EMT truck were parked. Heidi anxiously paced there, awaiting the EMTs' return. What an excruciating wait it must have been.

The EMTs' side of the story is that, after arriving at the yurt area, the 9-1-1-calling hiker had guided them up the hill from the camp base. I wonder if the EMTs struggled finding the IAB trailhead as I had earlier. No matter. These two EMTs humped a mobile medical gurney and equipment up the hill to my location in a record ten to twelve minutes, about the same time as it had taken me on the bike, and had done it with about eighty to one hundred pounds of equipment. I thank God these Iron Man studs arrived as quickly as they did! I'm sure that, during the challenge of IAB hill, the "I'm not a wiener but a manly man" syndrome provided these heroes ample motivation, especially if they could save a life. I cannot think of any more gratifying accomplishment than saving a life, and they dedicate their training to the credo "We save lives."

Even with daily training sessions, followed by mundane emergency responses, these guys never know when any portion of their training might make a split-second difference between life and death. This day, of all days, would test their physical stamina, their medical-first-responder skills, and their Danica Patrick driving skills. In true Yogi Berra "It ain't over 'til it's over" fashion, they went to work.

As they broke out their equipment and made their assessment, they realized that I was unresponsive and in AFib (as in, the heart is quivering or has an irregular heartbeat called arrhythmia). AFib is an indicator of a myocardial infraction, the fancy wording doctors hide behind meaning "big heart attack." At this stage, it can lead to stroke, heart failure, and other bad stuff. The EMTs knew the clock was running out, and every second counted, if "we save lives" was to mean anything.

The EMTs immediately began CPR, using the portable AED several times to re-sync my heartbeat. These were King County trained firefighters and EMTs using the latest 100–120 compressions per minute, thirty compressions followed by two breaths CPR procedures, while breaking out AED, universal protection, and whatever other magical gear they'd humped up for the mile long and 500-foot-high climb.

Later, I learn that King County's training has resulted in it leading the country in heart attack/CPR saves. For every one hundred cardiac-arrest calls, an additional thirteen patients will live under their care. I have no doubt that, if it were not for the Carnation and Fall City EMTs, someone would have written an obituary about me that would have included mountain-trail biking and IAB hill.

Seemingly stable after their initial response, the EMTs loaded me onto what passed as a backcountry gurney and began the excruciatingly slow return down the hill, because nowhere was there space to land a helicopter. Time was of the essence. My heart was periodically going into AFib, requiring AED jolts, and unknown damage to the heart was occurring.

"Stop the gurney; he's in AFib!"
"Clear!"
BAM!
"Sinus rhythm…"

"Stop the gurney; he's in AFib!"
"Clear!"
BAM!
"Sinus rhythm…."

Again, and again, and again….

Their arms aching, their legs burning, their lungs sucking the air for any added oxygen, these Iron Men took me down IAB to the yurt area, where another set of EMTs took over transporting me over twenty miles to the nearest cardio trauma center in Bellevue, Washington.

At some point, Heidi tells me that the EMTs would not allow her to ride in the ambulance, and she could see the desperation and sadness in their eyes and their body language, sending her a clear message: *"We don't think he is going to make it."* I know Heidi was praying on her rosary while following that ambulance to the hospital emergency-room entrance. She was probably thinking back to the little spat we'd had earlier that morning and how I'd stopped by her clinic to see her before the bike ride, with a Starbucks coffee and a card. Knowing her, she was probably thinking, *"Did I genuinely thank him and tell him I loved him? What were our last words? Stop it. God will see us through."*

I think back to the raw fear Heidi must have felt, watching this unfold and following that ambulance to Bellevue. I'm not sure which is worse, the heart attack or pondering the consequences as a detached observer, praying for your spouse of twenty-five-plus years. *"Is he going to live? Will he be the same? Did I tell him I loved him in our last conversation this morning? How do I tell the boys? What do I do if .... oh God, please!"* At this point, on the way to the hospital, it had been an hour and fifteen minutes since the two hikers had found me. Her nursing mind would have been kicking into overdrive, interspersed with knife-piercing thoughts of the consequences of brain hypoxia and heart damage. *"This cannot be happening!"*

From the top of IAB until they got me to the emergency room, the EMTs repeated the "AFib, clear, BAM, sinus rhythm" pattern twenty-five times. This was life and death, my life and death, and those steely-eyed professionals were not about to give up until the doctor made a pronouncement. Grit, resolve, refusal to give up, near exhaustion from humping equipment and a dying man down a mountain.... Where do they find people like this? You have got to hand it to these guys, not only for the endless training and attention to detail but for also their sheer determination. *"He's got a chance, if we can do this in time. This ain't happening, not on my watch."*

Try to remember these first responders the next time they are "passing the boot," or even if they are selling a male or female firefighter calendar. With pure, unadulterated, gritty resolve, and subject-matter expertise, these physical specimens, the firefighters and EMTs, live for the save and are crushed when it doesn't work out. It's not simply a lost game where you shake hands afterward and walk away. This ain't the Superbowl. This is real life, and losing a patient never goes away. Nightmares can last forever.

Can you imagine how impactful traumatic events are to first responders? Employees may be mindful of leaving unfinished work behind—the unfinished spreadsheet that was due yesterday, the unfinished project, the unfilled order, or whatever. They may have pangs of regret while safe at home late at night watching TV. But think of the first responder who held a dying baby in his hands, taking her last breath, or the ER nurse finishing a twelve-hour shift where some ten trauma patients passed through during her shift. Once you've seen a traumatic event or a mangled patient, it's impossible to unsee it. Where can you release those experiences? What can bring you back? No wonder we see increases in PTSD, drug and alcohol abuse (or worse) in the first-responder population. No wonder first responders are so dedicated to "saving lives, one life at a time."

Again and again, with no let up, these guys brought me back from the abyss. "Failure is not an option." "It ain't over till it's over." Then they handed me off to the emergency-room nurses, who assessed me again, awaiting the on-duty heart surgeon. But wait....

"He's in AFib!"

"Clear!"

BAM!

"Sinus rhythm..."

Again, and again, and again…

I was shocked another twenty times in the ER. So, you anal-retentive school graduates, yes, you counted right. I got more than forty-five shocks. Talk about gritty, "never give up" medical personnel! Got to love those guys.

(Side note: I think Heidi wants an accessible, remote-controlled AED to help improve my behavior. I bet there's an iPhone app.)

Diagnostic tests reveal that my left atrial descending artery, LAD for short (or in layman's terms, "the widow maker") is almost completely blocked, with considerable heart swelling. The ER team does note, however, possible "collateral flow," which means that veins have developed around and outside of the LAD blockage. The cardiac surgeon recommends thera-peutic hypothermia, the process of cooling the body's core temperature to preserve and/or prevent brain and additional heart damage. (Some might dispute whether I managed full brain recovery, but I think I survived with minimal brain damage overall.) The LAD blockage would be taken care of by inserting a stent a couple of days later during surgery.

I was oblivious to all this, of course, as I was in an induced coma, during which time Heidi asks our priest to visit me. I know it helped her more than me, due to my aforementioned oblivion. I admire Heidi's faith. Always have. I stopped going to church when I went off to college, not because I stopped believing but more because, as a twenty-year-old, I was self-centered, believed I was infallible, and thought I needed no one. I don't think it's unusual for young men and women to think this way, because they usually enjoy good health, are independent, and perhaps have had few (if any) traumatic life experiences or disappointments. Like opening day of the base-ball season, at twenty years old, you have a perfect record. No defeats. As you grow older, you remember the lessons learned from the defeats, but at that point in your life, you can do anything; you are infallible.

Everyone probably goes through a period of feeling independent and in charge. God works mysteriously, and I started going back to church not because of piety but because of Heidi's evening-shift work schedule of Tuesday through Saturday. The initial once-a-week dates revolved around enjoying Sunday brunches after listening to her sing in the choir. I'm sure God was working in the background thinking, *"If you won't come to me on your own, I'll get you back to me in a different way."* Having four sons you are so proud of will also certainly change you from a self-centered twenty-year-old hot-shot to a proud father.

The cardiac surgeon did a phenomenal job, but it is like taking your car to a mechanic. It is back in working order, but you have no idea what went on under the hood. Think about this surgeon, or any surgeon for that matter, and the tremendous amount of pressure they must be under to perform. I mean, nobody is going to a surgeon who gets it right "most" of the time. Luckily, we no longer need to crack open chests to work on hearts, which reduces the body's shock and recovery time. If you can believe it, the surgeons reach the heart by going through the groin area, the femoral artery. Nearest I can tell, the angioplasty/stent procedure goes like this:

- Performed through an artery in your groin.
- Given a sedative, which puts you out.
- Administered fluids, general medications, and blood-thinning medications (anticoagulants) through an IV catheter.
- Heart rate, pulse, blood pressure, and oxygen levels are monitored during the procedure.

- The doctor prepares the area (groin) with an antiseptic solution and places a sterile sheet.
- A small, thin guidewire is then inserted in the blood vessel.
- With the help of live X-rays, the doctor threads a thin tube (catheter) through your artery.
- Contrast dye is injected through the catheter once it's in place. This allows the doctor to see the inside of your blood vessels and identify the blockage on X-ray images called angiograms.
- A small balloon with a stent at the tip of the catheter is inflated at the left anterior descending vein, widening the blocked artery. After the artery is stretched, a stent is placed at the constricted site, the balloon is deflated, and the catheter is removed.

The procedure takes several hours, depending on the difficulty and number of blockages and whether any complications arise.

After awakening several days later, and out of stent surgery, the nurses start me on a limited therapy routine of walking down the corridors and the use of an hourly aspirator tube to prevent pneumonia. The aspirator is a tubular device, which you blow into at a specific rate to suspend a small ball with the pressure of your breath. The aspirator tube is sheer torture to blow into but essential to limiting lung-fluid buildup and possible pneumonia. Tongue in cheek, Nurse Ratchet, from the movie *One Flew Over The Cuckoo's Nest*, has nothing on these RNs, but I guess it was tough-love time. Of course, at this point, I am still relying on humor to cover up my concern, asking if my patient bracelet allows me into the beer tent. But Nurse Ratchet had nothing on Heidi:

"You need to get up, you need to walk, and you need to blow in the aspirator."

To which I replied, "I don't need this kind of abuse. I can get this at home." Yeah, sometimes the irreverent humor cover-up can hurt people and that one was harsh.

Over the course of a few days, several of the participating EMTs on subsequent patient deliveries are stunned to find out about me, and in typical firefighter/EMT fashion, they relay back to the station, "Hey, that 'It's A Bitch' biker is still kicking. WTH!"

I have learned through my firefighter/EMT niece how they seemingly remain detached from expressing their emotions, and that they, like me, hide their emotions through comedy, sarcasm, and jibes. The emotional outlet comes in guarded measures in front of significant others, occasional mandatory counseling, or worse, through drug and/or alcohol abuse. First responders do not get much appreciation, but when someone can relay a story about a "save," it has to be a rewarding feeling. A few months later, Heidi and I arranged to meet the responders at their firehouse with sandwiches, cupcakes, and cake. It was cathartic for all of us, and I shared some thank-you tears for sure. I wonder how many people actually thank first responders and medical personnel. I resolve to continue showing them gratitude when I can.

You know, when I think back on those firefighters and EMTs, they remind me of my father-in-law, who has passed away. I remember a simple, honest, hardworking, and proud German. His hands always struck me—those gnarled, calloused hands. The left hand was missing three fingers, evidently from a momentary lapse while using an electric saw. He did not lose them intentionally, foolishly, or from carelessly arriving at work with a hangover or drug-induced stupor. He had been a proud carpenter for years and probably the repetitive, onerous drudge of routine work caused a momentary distraction.

I admired his precision, his desire for keeping everything in its place and having a place for everything. His style was squares, rectangles, and straight lines—simple, honest, no subterfuge. Except, that one fateful day, there was one little tiny lapse. Maybe he was thinking of his problems. Did the saw bind in the wood? Did it hit a knothole? Or did someone bump into him? We will never know, but in that instant, the saw ripped through his middle, ring, and pinky fingers on his left hand. So where am I going with this? Losing his fingers was bad, but he dealt with it. His philosophy said, "These are the cards I was dealt, so what's next?" At this point, my cards were still being dealt.

I think about how the firefighter and EMTs can have that one perilous, momentary distraction and the dangerous consequences that might transpire. Hundreds of innocuous responses until the one time when every second of training and experience comes into play. Training scenarios never play out like real scenes, because in training, you can stop the scenario and discuss the action, but not on a mountainside, thirty minutes from the nearest hospital. Realistic scenarios in "game time" situations are the ultimate in training sessions.

These are the same conditions we confronted when designing scenarios in our pilot-training department when I was an instructor pilot, as well as the similar conditions we find with the athletic teams I work with now. Put on the pressure to perform in order to see the level of comprehension and skill acquired during each of the practice segments. Does the training transfer to real situations? Commercial aviation actually changed the training philosophy starting some twenty-five years ago from "perform this set of skills" to learning scenarios played out in real time.

In the past, simulator rides consisted of takeoffs, rejected takeoffs, engine failure on takeoff, approaches with an engine shutdown, missed approaches, and more, all presented in neatly packaged segments to minimize the training time required. We found, however, that these training segments did not transfer to actual situations, hence the philosophical change. The new and improved training philosophy still spends time on similar training segments, but now, the employees' scenarios play out in real time. The realism extends to actual use of all aircraft equipment, actual interphone calls from flight attendants, and diversions to non-standard airports and runways. Incorporating crew-resource management, the benefits from the injected realism allows training and learning to occur under stress and pressure to the point where learning outcomes become nearly real experiences. I like to think that the EMTs' real-time training scenarios were like our pilot simulators—pressure situations, challenging your repertoire and performance with real decisions and execution.

Similarly, baseball practices (Have I mentioned I coach baseball?) need real-time pressure game-situation segments. Batting practice where all hits need to go to the right side of the infield, double-play practice in different fielding scenarios and counted in how many can be completed in three minutes, or scrimmages with baserunners in scoring position, are all pressure-packed practice scenarios promoting real-time play.

Instruction periods remain essential building blocks, but more and more, creating realistic scenarios played out in real time, with authentic pressures and decisions, make the best teaching moments, and those proverbial "aha" moments occur more frequently. My point is that these EMTs most assuredly referred back to their heart-attack scenarios, performing CPR with no definitive end point. I don't know if you have gone through CPR training, but performing chest compressions for five minutes is exhausting, even if you have a partner to trade rest periods with you. Imagine performing chest compressions for thirty to sixty minutes to save an actual life, and having to hump a gurney three to four miles on a mountain trail. There can be no end to the appreciation I can extend to those EMTs.

The days since my heart problem are still a blur, consisting mostly of RNs administering doctors' orders. The medical people went in and out of my room almost like WWF tag-team wrestlers tagging in and out of the ring. The doctors blow in and out of the room with the usual questions—insincere ones like, "How are *we* feeling today" or inane ones like, "So, what are you in for?" I guess they ask these to see if I am coherent or aware of the situation, but isn't there a better question set? I should have answered, "I'm feeling good, but I am not sure about you, doc!" or "I'm in for a hangnail."

The nurses, however, were a different story. You could not ask for a more empathic group, even if they did torture me with hall walks and aspirator exercises. I wonder if nurses have to try to be empathic or if it just comes naturally. Hmmm, I have to contemplate that some other time. My biggest regret is not remembering and thanking every nurse that came in contact with me. I wish I could personally write them a note, one along the lines of, "Thank you for your compassion and caring. You made a difference." But if I saw them personally, the knuckle-dragging Neanderthal who hides behind humor would say, "Thanks from the heart of my bottom."

After six days in the hospital, I'm sent home. You know how it is; the insurance companies and hospitals are optimizing resources. But breathing and moving are still tortuous. I can't sleep, even sitting up, because breathing is so difficult. No one knew, but my left lung was slowly filling with fluid. After eighteen hours at home, Heidi decides I need to return to the hospital, because something ain't right. I remain on the medical floor for another couple of days and seem to be improving again, but not before telling the primary nurse that, if something happened, she was cleared for "artificial recreation" but needed to remember that "I *am* happily married." I'm finally sent home. Maybe, I was told, "You are bothering the nurses too much. Go home." I don't remember. Discharge instructions ask me to see my new friend, the cardiologist, in three days.

3 – REHAB

"You can find hope in despair. Dwell on positive thoughts."
—Lailah Gifty Akita

I return to the medical building near the hospital to be assessed by my new cardiac-doctor friend, but he is busy with another patient. So, a nurse practitioner (NP) does her assessment, and she decides to get a closer look at my lungs via a CT scan. She discovers fluid in my left lung. In modern-day medicine, NPs and RNs do most of the assessments it seems, and this NP is an incredibly empathic, knowledgeable medical practitioner. The fact is that the lung has considerable fluid. She tells me a compromised heart with partial lung function (pleural effusion) can cause you to feel bad. *No sh*t!*

So now the NP, with the cardiologist's approval, sends me to have my lung drained. This is a tricky procedure, requiring the insertion of a tube between two ribs in your back, and there is little they can do to decrease the pain except some localized anesthesia. Enduring the pain, I sit bolt upright in a dead sweat, enduring waves of aching pain. The nurse reaches over, placing a soothing wet cloth on my neck, and I ask her name. She tells me it's Kathy (not her real name), and suavely, in my most sincere babe-magnet voice, I say, "Kathy, I love you."

Drained of about a liter of liquid I-don't-know-what, I'm a new man. Who knew your body needs all that oxygen to feel good? *Oxygen ... we don't need no stinkin' oxygen.* To paraphrase

Yogi Berra, "They also thoroughly examined my head and didn't find anything."

Since I'm feeling stronger, my cardiologist is ready to schedule the placement of an implantable cardioverter defibrillator (ICD), which occurs in late December, some two months after my heart event. The American Heart Association describes an ICD as "a battery-powered device placed under the skin that keeps track of your heart rate and may pace your heart when needed." Thin wires connect the ICD to your heart. If an abnormal heart rhythm is detected—beating chaotically or much too fast—the device will deliver an electric shock to restore a normal heartbeat. *Well, I'm not going to need it, because I'm going to work out and get stronger, but if the doc recommends it, I can deal with it.* It seems Heidi is getting her wish for a shock-collar behavioral-modification device, or BMD.

The placement is done via surgery under general anesthesia. The ICD is described as a stopwatch-size device placed subcutaneously (Isn't it easier to say "under the skin?") just below the collarbone. The hard part is placing the electrical leads into specific heart parts. Possible risks include excessive bleeding, damage to blood vessels at the catheter insertion site, infection, tearing of the heart muscle, and a collapsed lung. The list goes on to say, "If you are pregnant or think you are pregnant, or currently breastfeeding...." So, let me add DEATH again to the side-effect list. I mean really? The risks sound like the average TV advertisement for the latest drug, don't they? Anyway, I have one implanted and supposedly have a ninety-five percent chance of surviving another heart attack as I tote my own private AED.

Heidi was a rock, as always, advocating, cajoling, and basically kicking butt. When it comes to protecting family, husband, and kids, she puts a lioness protecting her cubs to shame. But I can see cracks in the façade as the days drag into weeks and months. Palpable concern is safely hidden, but I can see it wearing her down. Thoughts of permanent care, loss of spouse, four boys and college, mortgage, and income are all racing in her mind. Buddhist monks refer to controlling your "monkey mind," but they are men and don't realize how women work through problems by spilling out all the emotional reasoning.

Intelligence is measured in a variety of ways. Your intelligence quotient (IQ) is one of the most common data points. Popular sentiment does not acknowledge the other side of intelligence. Emotions and intuition play a bigger role than most people think. Your emotional quotient, or EQ if you will, on top of any logic and intuition, plays a huge role in decision-making. Women are decidedly better at using their EQ in decisions, not because of better capability but because they more readily accept EQ inputs and are more comfortable in expressing their feelings. I have a brother who expressed it this way: "I don't do emotions." So maybe Buddhist monks, men, should not downplay emotional reasoning or "monkey mind." That will be a great discussion topic the next time I'm in the Himalayas in the lotus position becoming one with the universe with my designated guru.

Heidi did her best to get me back on track—back to some sort of semblance of moving toward acceptance and the future. Someone once told me that there are a thousand ways of doing things right and only three or four of doing them wrong. Indecision is one of the wrong ways. Indecision is really a default way of saying, "I don't know what to do," which lets the event completely control the outcome. She repeated an oft-used quote: "The roads are full of flattened squirrels who couldn't make up their minds which way to go." Heidi started moving forward with "what's important next" with the help of her mother, who came out from Chicago to Seattle to help my recuperation and rehab.

Heidi asked her to come out and help because she needed to return to work, and we were not sure when, or if, I would do the same. I had plenty of sick leave, but Heidi had none. I am sure it was a difficult decision to return to work while I was rehabilitating. Besides, losing her income would impact plans for four boys' college tuitions, as would my now-possible forced retirement. I will forever be indebted to my mother-in-law for the help and aid she provided during my rehabilitation. Like her daughter, an RN by profession, my mother-in-law watched, assessed, fixed food, and prompted me to move about.

I lost a considerable amount of weight, some twenty-five pounds, and my appetite was gone. I could easily lose twenty-five pounds now and not look sickly, but twenty-five pounds twelve years ago? That was tough. Nutrition and fluids were an important part of rehab, and she made sure I ate and drank. She made some of the simplest and tastiest soups, which became my staple for a while. Who knew pancake soup would become a house specialty? Gradually, I started gaining lost weight back, and unfortunately, I continue the weight gain trend to this day. There is little danger I will be the "before and after" spokesperson for Nutrisystem or Weight Watchers.

4 – YOU ONLY HURT
THE ONES

"Our prime purpose in this life is to help others. And if you can't help them, at least don't hurt them."
—Dalai Lama

During this entire time, I had not thought of the effect my experience was having on my four sons, whose ages were twelve, seventeen, twenty-one, and twenty-three at the time. I can only imagine how profound the shock (no pun intended) was of seeing their dad in an induced coma. I was the guy ... THE GUY. I think back on my father's diagnosis of lung cancer and the short two months he had following it. My dad, THE GUY I depended on for advice, the love-tough guy (because love should always come first) would not make it. In the last coherent conversation I had with my dad, he advised me to take care of the people closest to me, the important ones defined as the ones who would attend your funeral service, not the acquaintances and work associates.

It is said that you are the sum total of the five people with whom you surround yourself most (not including your family). Nelson Mandela used the Bantu word *"Ubuntu,"* (I am because we are) as a rallying cry against South African apartheid. What a perfect word for those around you who define you, a rallying cry entwined in a hidden thank you: "Ubuntu." The important people around us—family and the five people we surround ourselves with—make us who we are, and for sure, those are the ones with whom you have you deep conversations and who show up at your funeral.

After this conversation, my dad went through the radiation and chemotherapy treatments, which rapidly sapped his strength, endurance, care, and willpower. The treatments drain you physically but a certain fear of your own morality also causes you to turn inward, shutting down your logical, intuitive Jedi spirit and turning up that certain reptilian instinct for self-survival. You know how a reptile's only concern is food, water, hot, and cold? This does not exactly exude warm feelings. I mean, when have you ever heard someone talk about curling up on the couch with a bag of popcorn to watch a movie with his pet iguana? Dad's brain was in reptilian mode—protection, comfort, and survival, with no regard for others' feelings, but we all knew a battle raged inside his body and mind.

Once serious chemo treatment starts (Are there any less-than serious?), most times the humanness starts to leave and basic survival sets in. That was my dad, frenetic pacing, not sleeping for fear of never waking, and inconsolable. It was a long, painful goodbye with my dad, as opposed to what my sons were contemplating: either a sudden or fairly quick demise for me, with no chance at a final conversation or a long goodbye. The sudden event caused frantic memory searches about the last conversations they'd had with Dad. Was it a one-on-one, pre-school breakfast or a few beers at our favorite watering hole? The sudden realization that their dad may be gone must have weighed heavy.

The realization affected them all equally. Worry and stress manifested in all of them in one way or another. The very suddenness, as opposed to a long goodbye, becomes a Gordian knot. Neither the "slow progression toward death" nor sudden death is really much better than the other, with good and bad options with either, but it was what it was. "Deal with it." They did. Helping my Mom, Betty, became a top priority. Doing what you're supposed to do and a little more, circling the wagons, and supporting each other intuitively became prime directives. The little voices in their heads, remembering what they'd once considered trifle "Dad-isms," were reflexively echoing between their ears.

Mutual support is a theme my wife and I instill deeply in our sons. Our family watches over and keeps up with each other on an almost daily basis. When one of us needs support, support becomes a priority. Each can ask any one other of us for a discussion without judgment or punishment, a designated "free to express" talk, or a time-out talk. As far back as when our first son started school, I periodically took each one to breakfast prior to the start of school, just to talk. Whether the topic was serious or turned into a discussion of whether King Kong could defeat Godzilla, every talk was important. I don't know how this got started, but we enjoyed the breakfasts so much that we continue them today in a slightly different way. Instead of breakfast, we regularly get together one-on-one for a couple of beers and some buffalo wild wings.

The German tradition of getting together periodically with family and/or friends is called a *stammtisch,* or "non-structured, traditionally social meeting marked with a somewhat elaborate sign reserving it for regulars." I think *stammtisch* keeps the boys and me centered and involved with each other, while also offering each of us a built-in sounding board.

Brené Brown, in her book *Dare to Lead,* emphatically notes that nothing creates better relationship bonds than sharing vulnerability and trust between leaders and teams. Both vulnerability and trust are keystones not only for servant leadership but also for building strong, caring relationships. All my sons have the empathy gene from their mother, and yet have character enough to embrace accountability, responsibility, and love. The very essence and purpose of family is support while promoting love, kindness, and happiness. My family was, is, and will always be my top priority, and we will always be there for each other. Nowhere is it more evident than at our *stammtisches,* where Heidi may occasionally appear. Having Heidi does not really change the dynamic either. After thirty-six years of marriage and four boys, she readily joins in the "smack talk" with short, little, wicked retorts that have us howling with laughter.

Our four sons are admirable and talented. I mean, I have been with each of them since they entered the world as five- to eight-pound, little, wrinkled raisins. They rely on each other for support. Sure, momentary sibling rivalries slip in, but they are the very definition of brotherhood. Some of the rivalries center around which IPA is the best, why the b-roll on *Rocketman* could have had better cutaways, or the FX shots in *Jumanji* needing better CGI. "Can't we just enjoy the movie?" When it comes down to sounding boards though, they have each other's back for sure. Still this Dad stuff really hit them hard, and was literally too close to home. How is it that one day we deal with daily trifles and the next is a life changer? Deal with this moment and learn from the past, for the best is yet to come.

In an amazing coincidence, the morning of my heart attack, I had a great conversation with my mother, almost prescient considering what would happen later on the bike ride. I was in a reflective mood, so during the conversation, I mentioned how, throughout most of my life, I had tried to imitate my dad and felt I had inherited a lot of his traits. I went on to tell her about how I came to realize I was really most like her. The humor, the empathy, and the importance of relationships are part of my mother's personality. We were laughing together as

I reminisced about the family gathering for her eightieth birthday. Once all the family arrived, my mom brought out Jell-O shots for everyone, at least the ones who were of drinking age.

See, my mother has a unique combination of traits we could all learn from. It's not like she lives by a river in Egypt, affectionately referred to as the Dee Nile (denial); rather, she sets about finding the good in any situation or in any person. She can connect with any group, as long as they are near enough to talk. I remember going to a wine festival one time when we lived outside of Athens, Greece, at one of my Air Force father's base assignments. As we laid out a picnic blanket and gathered our wine samples, bread, cheese, and assorted picnic fare, she had already struck up a conversation with a group of Brits next to us. Brits are stereotypically reserved and sometimes less than welcoming to strangers. No matter, my mom had already connected with them, offering up a toast to "The Colonies" and the festival added to our family's sagas.

Little did I know the effect my heart attack would have on my mother. Unintentionally, we sometimes hurt the ones we love. While a certain degree of denial did set in, I think she was devastated to realize she might lose a child. The rule is that a mother is supposed to go to heaven before her child, but contemplating me going first was a difficult concept to wrap her head around, much less for the skeptical people doubting my qualifications to enter to heaven. I'm her child, and that is how she still thinks of me. Even now, at sixty-seven years old, I'm a twenty-year-old hotshot needing guidance. I still reverently defer to her for advice. She is older, and undoubtedly smarter, and there is still a comfort knowing Mom loves and cares for her son. She always tells me that she prays for me. Heidi probably tells her I could use even more prayers. You could not ask for more from someone who lives a thousand miles away.

What can I add? The heart attack was definitely out of my control, but I cannot help thinking about its effects on my wife, sons, my own family, and the five people I surround myself with all the time. The fine line between intentionally inflicted hurt and unintentional, unplanned hurt makes no difference to the recipient. Strangers do not care and take little heed, but if you know the ones you hurt ... well, you only hurt the ones you love.

5 – FREE YOUR SPIRIT

"There is strange comfort in knowing no matter what happened today, the sun will rise again tomorrow."
—Aaron Lauritsen

Weeks go by with my rehab sessions, including stints on the treadmill, the stationary bike, and lifting weights, and I'm learning to recognize my cardio limitations without the wireless EKG monitors worn during the workouts. The ten rehab patients and I cannot just enter the center to begin our regimen. The requirement is to gown up after having EKG-type leads stuck to our chests, which are connected to transmitting boxes attached to our waist belts. Then we have a quick ten- to fifteen-minute presentation and discussion about cardiac care. Finally, we get to a W.O.D. (workout for the day).

The therapists are on top of monitoring me through the wireless sensors strapped to my body. Each time I press the limits, the therapists react with stern admonition to slow down. I am making progress, feeling almost normal, and thinking I might be able to return to work and flying sooner than everyone thinks. Moving the needle on your "personal record" (PR for the triathlete types) is how we improve our endurance, right? I am dumbfounded with the therapists' restrictions, and I momentarily think, *Did I miss something in the confusion of medical appointments, Lexiscans, and discharge instructions?* You cannot always stay positive all the time. There was a gap between "Pollyanna" positive and the reality that was occurring, unbeknownst to me. I figured the therapists should be cutting me loose soon, because no "legitimate tough guy" (LTG) can stay under 135 heart beats per minute or have to worry about blood pressure and still strive for a PR in stationary cycling or Olympic treadmill events.

I reflect back at my mid-December doctor visit and the nuclear stress test. *What the heck? I'm not the Manhattan Project, and he's not Doctor Oppenheimer.* Here's the cardiologist's explanation: "A nuclear exercise stress test is a diagnostic test used to evaluate blood flow to and from the heart. During the test, a small amount of radioactive tracer is injected into a vein. A special camera, called a gamma camera, detects the radiation released by the tracer to produce computer images, and cardiologists are able to measure heart efficiency by measuring the ratio of blood input and output. At rest and during exertion, the gamma camera images show areas of poor blood flow and damaged areas." I remember this part of the conversation, but at the time, I was not in the best of physical or mental condition and I miss a key part of the doctor's spiel about not returning to fly ever again. What I missed would play a key part in a future doctor visit.

Interestingly, during the test, you walk on a treadmill while increasing the speed and grade until you reach your exertion limit, hence the moniker "stress test." *Wait … isn't this how I got here in the first place? By increasing my speed and climb grade? If they start showing hiking images on a video of "It's A Bitch," we are going to have words.*

Prior to the test, I'm getting assessed by the nurse practitioner (NP) with all the usual "How you feeling? How you doing?" questions. We get beyond the "What are you in here for today" question. I'm feeling great, doing well, and I'm ready for the doctor to release me back to flying. I don't notice the quizzical look on the NP's face. In retrospect, the look was an omen. I completed the approximately one-hour test, and I'm sitting with the cardiologist, looking at the recorded video on a computer monitor. It's sort of a Mario Kart, Xbox video tour on steroids, as you watch a replay of blood pumping through the heart chambers—way cool visuals of two atria, two ventricles, a tricuspid, pulmonary, mitral, and aortic valve, and an enlarged heart due to the damage.... Then the conversation turns way serious.

The doctor asks, "You do know that your ejection fraction is reduced from normal?"

"Hmmm. No, I didn't. What is that anyway?"

"Yes, that's the ratio of the entering blood amount to that which is pumped out. The normal range is about fifty to seventy-five percent. Anything under forty percent is indicative of extensive heart damage."

"What's mine?"

"Well, yours is twenty-five percent."

"Wow, that's not great, but I'll keep working out and get my heart back in shape." A Kung Fu truism comes to mind as I read the doctor's body language: *Not so fast, little grasshopper, you must become one with your destiny.* The cardiac talk goes on, and the doc communicates matter-of-factly that the ICD will be permanent and is the reason you'll be prevented from flying barring new developments in stem-cell research and heart-tissue repair ... blah, blah, blah.

I'm only half hearing as I am completely stunned, and I realize for the first time that I'm *never* going to fly again. Ever. My last day flying was October 12, 2008, flying a day turn from Seattle to San Diego and back, and I didn't even know it. No pictures, no Heidi in first class, and no nice layover somewhere. The reality sets in. For sure, I won't be flying at 35,000 feet, looking down at the people below looking up at me saying, "Hey, look at those guys up there flying around."

They say that, if you love your job, you will never work a day. I don't know what to say to the doctor. I have never been as stunned as I am at that moment. A lump grows in my throat, a stinging sensation pierces the corners of my eyes, my head bows, and I choke out the words, "You mean...." I can't get the words to come out. There's only a huge lump in my throat and a quiet sob as I hear him continue.

"Yes, it's serious, but most people with this type of heart condition can expect to live upwards of eight to ten years, and flying ... well, you've flown your last flight as a pilot. Do you understand what I am saying?" Brutal, naked truth with no accompanying comforting barely registers as I choke back the urge to question his and his mother's lineage.

Where's Heidi? I need Heidi, stat. I keep thinking, *You mean, I can't make it better? It's not in my control? I mean ... noooo! Come on, if I just work harder, maybe ... noooo, this can't be! I will work harder at rehab. C'mon, man!*

No one, except another pilot, can understand the crushing blow of not flying again. It is hard enough facing not flying when you reach the planned, mandatory retirement age. The years of study and practical training go by the wayside. The hours away from home, missed family events, red-eye flights, the challenges, the twice-yearly physicals, check rides, and Air Force deployments all come down to a heartless (no pun intended) realization: "Your services are no longer needed." I know I can still function as a pilot, but the odds of another heart attack with passengers onboard is a risk no one wants to take. No final flight, firetruck spray, taxiing-in, overnight at your favorite layover city with your wife. It's all simply wiped away. And ... *AND* ... your skills are so specialized that they are not readily transferrable, except maybe as a beta tester for an Xbox flying game.

Driving away, it takes a while to absorb the shock before I start replaying the conversation in my mind. Yes, he basically said I would have to quit flying nine years before mandatory FAA retirement at sixty-five years old. Wait … what was that part about I could expect to live upwards of eight to ten years? Was he serious? Is that quality years or a flat eight to ten years?

I relate the conversation with Heidi and get to the life-expectancy part, and she just about blows a gasket. "He has no right and no basis for saying that! I'm going to call him and set him straight! Where does he get off with that statement?" On and on and on she vents. I tell her to let it go; it won't change anything anyway. H*ll has no fury like Heidi's family disparaged, especially her boys—all five of us! Well, my fingers are crossed, but it's been twelve years, and like an Energizer Bunny, I keep going.

Not medically trained, I took a while to accept Heidi's assessment of post-traumatic stress syndrome (PTSD). I would never compare my situation to the trauma returning soldiers go through, especially those who have been wounded or witnessed horrific events. Nonetheless, I regret my dismissive comments to Heidi when she mentioned it, but as usual, she knows more than I do about medicine, and my recovery does fit into a type of PTSD.

My memory of the heart attack and initial few days is completely erased, yet every so often, I have flashbacks, nightmares, or reminders with small heart palpitations, causing me not-so-small concern. One poignant reminder is the claustrophobia I still experience every time my face is covered. It's a shame, because I use to enjoy snorkeling when I had an opportunity to do it, and as a previous pilot, I needed to wear an oxygen mask. Even a blanket across my face can cause a small panic as I get the claustrophobic feeling of warm, stale breath—a suffocating sensation.

I put off writing about my heart attack for almost twelve years, because every time I would start writing, my emotions would take over. I really had trouble drafting and editing the first few chapters of this book. Luckily, I had kept a lot of notes over the years and was able to quickly incorporate them. Counselors usually suggest journaling for trauma patients, and I guess in my independent, stubborn, knuckle-dragging Neanderthal way, I did it without admitting I was journaling. Don't tell anyone, but journaling is the manly way of keeping a diary. The journaling was (and is) my best outlet for "dealing with it."

Differentiating between possible PTSD symptoms and needing validation is hard to distinguish. Either way, if I have too much time to think, the negativity and feelings of isolation can take over. Most times, I still cannot discern the difference between the symptoms and my fear of premature "Geezerville." *"Geezerville – defined as that time in your life when a Bacarlounger, remote control and a cool drink become part of your daily routine."* When I am ready for it, I want "Geezerville" to be my life-changing choice, but who really knows what God has planned for us?

Another outlet for resolving to "deal with it" was working out three to four times per week, which eventually became routine. These are not the body-builder, beach body, maintain the six-pack-type workouts but rather the habit forming, "fit it within one hour" type, consisting of walking on the treadmill, arms, legs, and yoga stretching. I didn't succumb to yoga pants, because it would cause a distraction in any "hot yoga" class. Rest days, while needed, don't seem purposeful but nonetheless essential. There are times when the competitive twenty-year-old still comes out. About three years ago, after an indoor baseball practice, the team was doing sprints when they latched onto the idea of the coaches competing in the sprints.

It was not the brightest idea, considering my heart, but I did not finish last. The little voice in my head kept repeating, *"You shouldn't do this. This is not a good idea..."* and if Heidi knew ... omgosh.

The best part about the workouts was that they became routine. Some would argue that routine is boring, but I felt, in regards to my health and well-being, that becoming "Mr. Universe" or its equivalent, being featured in the firefighters' calendar, were no longer within reach. We've all read about centenarians who believed they reached their age by routine walks and a daily glass of red wine, or some similar recipe. My routine was the new reality, and I needed to deal with it. Besides, was it not Benjamin Franklin who said, "Wine is a constant proof that God loves us and loves to see us happy?" If you want to enjoy life, you need to have some health standards, but you need to free your spirit and live this moment too. My eighty-nine year old mom would be saying something like, "Let's make Jell-O shots!" Don't moms have simple solutions for everything?

USAF Academy graduation with Dennis' dad 1975.

*Circa 1977 Dennis standing on the entry ladder for
a student flight in a Northrop T-38.*

Circa 1985 Dennis and his oldest son on the flight deck of a Jet America MD-80.

Circa 1987 McDonnell-Douglas KC-10 in flight with the refueling boom down.

Dennis Mellen

Circa 1992 deploying to Taif, Saudi Arabia for Operation Restore Hope in Somalia bring food and supplies to the populace. Dennis is in front of McDonnell-Douglas KC-10 engine inlet.

Unknown file picture KC-10 and Northrop B-2.

KC-10 top-off with B-1, F-15s and F-22s.

Boeing 737 in Sitka, Alaska with Mount Edgecombe in the background.

Last Alaska Airlines McDonnell-Douglas MD-80 flight July 2008 with two Captains flying, myself and my boss in the left seat.

Coach Mel in full battle regalia 2015.

6 – WHAT'S IMPORTANT NEXT (W.I.N.)

"We must boldly advance into the shadows of uncertainty."
—Carl von Clausewitz

Once I was back home, and after a few weeks of deep depression, my wife was at a loss as to how to help. In desperation, she had me connect with a neighbor. We went through the same type of serious heart problems, so it actually helped. The deep funk I felt for weeks, the forlorn resignation, and the finality of "you won't fly again," much less live a long life, weighed heavy on my mind. I had several long discussions with this neighbor, and those talks helped me find my way back. He got me to think long term, as in find a new meaning. "Wad you gonna do?" became our familiar refrain.

I guess the analogy would be like going for a drive and deciding what your destination will be. Say, for instance, it's going to Disney World in Orlando, and you are driving from Chicago. There are literally hundreds of ways to get there—via Nashville, via Knoxville, or even via Atlanta, but just like your headlights have a certain range, you have to take care of the next two hundred feet, because you cannot see further than the headlight range, even though Disney World is still your goal. Take care of the next two hundred feet, take care of this moment. I asked myself, "Do you know where you are going?"

and the repetitive answer for too long was "I don't know. I don't know. I don't…."

I learned that I can take care of the next two hundred feet, because I can see that distance ahead. What I could not see was where to go after the next two hundred feet. *What is my big picture? Or better, what is my new North Star?* I was treading in new uncharted territory, because I had maintained a singleness in the purpose of being a career pilot since I was ten years old, and I had never explored new ideas before. I knew it would take time to sink into my head. At this point, I was not even sure of the questions to ask or what direction to move.

Those are the cards God dealt me. The Navy SEALs have a saying: "When things are not going as planned, when the uncontrollables outnumber the controllables, D.W.I.—deal with it." It took a few weeks of inconsolable depression for me to decide I had to start dealing with it, but my neighbor visited again and asked me what I was good at. I asked myself, "Can I go back to male hand modeling or should I be satisfied as Heidi's arm candy?" Oh well. "Fall down seven times, get up eight," as the old Japanese adage encourages.

It takes more than a fancy tagline or slogan to "deal with it." The feeling is similar to a baseball player in a slump. Some will try anything from voodoo dolls and changing bats to routine changes, or even checking with their mental-performance coach. I searched for my new meaning. One joke that makes the rounds of the baseball community is about a player checking in with his mentor, and it goes like this:

Player in slump: "What should I do?"

Old pro: "Switch from your 32-ounce bat to a 29-ounce bat."

Player: "Will that help?"

Old pro: "No, but it'll be lighter while you're carrying it back to the dugout."

I needed to close the holes in my game and change my career, but where to begin?

Truly, the "deal with it" process is a little complex and deeper than that, but humor can and should be a big part of it. The biggest obstacle in learning to deal with slumps, to deal with the situations, is as Coach Glen Pecoraro says: "Care less." Not careless, but "care less." Care less means to let go of the baggage, let go of what happened, and concentrate on this moment, and the influence you have in this moment. In a blog, the thread mentioned, "divine nonchalance," but "care less" is so much better. It is simple, and no one needs to use S.A.T. words if simpler works. I tried to get back into the zone and find my new purpose or role. "Care less" leads back to the zone. You've trained, you've practiced, and you've experienced similar situations. You literally go back into your brain's playbook and either use one of the plays you've mastered or come up with an alternative one, using a practiced play as a framework.

The movie *Top Gun* had a great scene and line, after Mav and Goose get chewed out by their boss, Viper, for the dangerous control-tower fly-by. Walking out of Viper's office, Goose says, "Thanks a lot, Mav. I really enjoyed that. Arrrgh! . . . Hey Mav, you still have that number for Truck Masters? I might need that." Talk about a classic D.W.I. (deal with it) line. Momentary remorse followed by "what's important next" is a great, forward-looking approach.

"So, Mel," I say to myself (a nickname I've become accustomed to) "so what? What's next?" I started the process of re-inventing myself. I started my "do over." Little did I know that the arduous, up and down, roller-coaster-ride job search I started that February day would last over a year. After all, I'm a fifty-six-year-old (at the time) master at flying—okay debatable—who is just a few short steps away from "Geezerville."

Fights on. I'm not ready to retire to the rocker, remote watching re-runs of *NYPD Blue* in the evenings and *Oprah* in the afternoons.

Author John Acuff comes to mind. He says, "Pivot don't panic; it's time to change versions of yourself, time to tap into your Career Savings Account, where you made deposits in your relationships, skills, character, and hustle." Ask yourself questions: Who do I know? What skills can I add? How can I show solid character, and hustle to provide a type of road map? I never had a problem with hustle. In baseball, the following skills and traits are reputed to require no talent by many coaches: being on time, work ethic, effort, body language, energy, attitude, passion, "coachability," doing extra, and being prepared, and feel I never had a problem with any of these. Patience is not my best quality. I exude more of a *get results now* kind of mentality, so I was looking for immediate results. The job search process is not like winning the lottery. It is a grind.

I became intimately familiar with Indeed, Glassdoor, and LinkedIn, likely applying to over three hundred different companies. All the while, I knew that it was an uphill struggle unless you get the silver bullet from someone you know. You don't get what you want by planning. You have to follow through and execute the plans. Acuff has it right: Dip into your Career Savings Account. Who do you know? What skills do you have? Use your hustle and work ethic.

Folklore uses the riddle about three crows sitting on a fence when one decides to fly south. The narrator then asks how many are left on the fence. The answer is three, because there is a difference between deciding and doing. It's time to do something. (Side note: The job I finally landed came through an indirect, online introduction after getting an email address while searching a company's contact list. Persistence, perseverance, grit. D.W.I.)

The life-changing transition did not happen easily and certainly not according to plan. Heavyweight-boxing champ Mike Tyson addressed plans this way: "Everyone has a plan until they get punched in the mouth." My punch in the mouth definitely changed my plans. Planning and plans have two completely different meanings. Planning is the process we go through for our future. A plan is what we started out with, but we adjust the plan according to the circumstances.

My planning started as early as ten years old, as I looked up at fighter planes flying above and got inspired to fly. I started *planning* the pathway to being a fighter pilot and a general in the Air Force. Reality steered me down a different pathway. Events occurred out of my control, which I could only influence with my responses. Toward the end of Air Force pilot training, we were asked to list our aircraft preferences for our initial assignments. My list included all fighters. Over half of Air Force pilot assignments are to cargo, transport, air-refueling tankers, and bombers due to the Air Force fleet make-up. While I was designated as fighter qualified, I was initially disappointed to be assigned to an air-refueling tanker. The disappointment was short-lived as I adjusted the plan and recommitted to a different career path. Just like General Dwight Eisenhower said: "No plan survives the first contact with the enemy." I needed to adjust my plan according to reality.

I did not have any idea which way events were pushing me, but I would not accept sitting idle, waiting for future events to unfold. Uncertainty loomed, casting a long shadow. My thoughts often drifted toward negativity, and I admonished myself continuously to stay positive. Everyone has negative thoughts: athletes, CEOs, and even counselors. Your mind wants to protect and preserve you. That mindset did well when we were pre-historic hunter-gathers living day-to-day. Back then, the survival instinct drove us to protect ourselves, and yesterday's threats were easily forgotten when today is another day to survive. Today, we tend to carry over yesterday's threats, events, and dangers like bricks in our pockets, weighing down our progress. "Drop the bricks," I tell myself. At the same time, the logical mind needs to remember the lessons of failure and drop the remorse for the failure.

Even the most optimistic among us has occasions of negativity; when there seems to be no end in sight, a person is bound to despair. It is important to turn the despair around. Have you ever witnessed a birthday party with one of those well-built piñatas, and no matter how hard the kids hit the piñata, it will not break open? Even after the blindfold is removed, and the kids can strategically aim their strikes, the piñata remains nearly intact. In exasperation, one of the adults intervenes with a mighty swing, and the piñata bursts open, sending candy everywhere. Stuck in the rut of negativity, maybe the easiest way out is through a friend intervening with a simple smile and gentle reminder. Or a not-so-gentle kick in the pants. All we can do is keep swinging at the piñata.

7 – HELP YOURSELF FIRST

"Never let success get to your head;
never let failure get to your heart."
—Anonymous

I can't sit very long. Job searching is not the most rewarding task, and progress is agonizingly slow and hard to measure, especially when feedback consists of "Two people have viewed your profile." Views, likes, and shares are not the best gauge of progress, nor are they indicators of genuine friends or genuine feedback. They are more like impersonal reminders to keep plugging away.

The situation prompted a corollary thought to the expression, "When leading a new team or organization, it will take longer to build a new culture if you allow negative people from the previous culture to contaminate the process." The corollary is that, if circumstances force a career change, do not let the negative event contaminate your search. Yes, I loved my previous job and never felt I worked a day, but the heart attack indeed ripped my heart out, threw it on the ground, and sent it through a food processor. Optimism was a distant concept, and depression sat on my shoulder like a parrot, constantly whispering negative thoughts in my ear. "You better be ready to hear some no's."

The days and job search rolled into seemingly monotonous routine. Not drudgery by any means, even if the time spent seemed without purpose. If I could have accepted

"Geezerville," it might have come easier; however, there was still a twenty-four-year-old hotshot with his hair on fire inside me looking for the next challenge. Simon Sinek describes the need like this: "Imagine a world where you wake up inspired, feel safe at work, and return home fulfilled at the end of the day ... because you know your why, your purpose." Mother Teresa knew her why and never regretted not having money, comfort, or material things. What is my new purpose? What is my *why*?

Knowing your *why*, your purpose, is important. Here's an allegory for knowing your *why:* A man is walking down the street when he comes upon a construction site. He approaches a bricklayer and asks, "What are you doing?" The bricklayer looks up but does not acknowledge the question. Walking further, the man comes upon another bricklayer and asks the same question: "What are you doing?"

The bricklayer answers, "I'm drawing a paycheck."

Walking up to a third bricklayer, the man again asks, "What are you doing?"

This bricklayer says, "I'm laying bricks for a beautiful cathedral, which will help feed the hungry and shelter some of the homeless."

Three bricklayers, one who does not care about anyone, one laying bricks for himself, and a third who has a purpose. Which one is inspired?

My concern—not a complaint—is that I could've arrived to the same point with a lot less effort. It explains, but doesn't slake, the ambition, the maverick, the Top Gun, the "need for speed," the need to be purposeful and validated. Finding my *why* was never a straight line. Maybe the bricklayer story has a fourth bricklayer: the one who seeks various cathedral-construction jobs, trying to find the one that fits, and settles on apprentice bricklaying because he can appreciate the progress on the cathedral as he masters his craft.

Why is it that when you have mastered your craft as a young person and want responsibility, you lack the experience to be trusted with the responsibility? And when you are old, you have the experience but are now too old for the responsibility? Think of the wasted knowledge, skills, and abilities of healthy fifty-five- to seventy-five-year-olds. That age group, and older even, would be content with a minimum of validation and get things done. I desperately needed a *why*—some sort of validation. "If you want something done, ask a busy person to do it," said Lucille Ball. I needed to be busy. I needed a reason and purpose.

Looking back, I feel there must be a reason God spared me. God means a lot to me, but I don't wear Him on my sleeve. Is that a good thing? I don't know, because I've never felt the evangelical need to push it onto other people. Is that a cop-out? Does that take away from living Christ-like? What I have embraced is serving others. For so long, I had too many commitments and an inverted priority list, and at this time of my life, I felt the need to make-up for lost opportunities and serve others. If the commitment was a decently paid leadership position, then servant leadership was a possibility. If it was a volunteer position, that would be okay too. I just needed to find the right venue.

Finding the right purpose, or the purpose God intends, is not the easiest thing to do. I had to remind myself to find the right pace. The right pace for a sprint race is different from the pace a runner uses for a distance race. God does not sit down with a couple of beers and talk with you, but He does talk to you through your friend's advice or in those quiet, contemplative times when you find yourself alone, meditating.

One day, I just looked up aviation schools and found one at Boeing Field—a high-school aviation and machine-shop school. Driving down the next day, I walked into what looked like a disheveled, run-down machine-shop-type building with several boarded windows. The building had not seen paint in twenty years. The paint of the building was chipping and weeds were growing at its base. The parking area also sorely needing repaving. It was almost a perfect location for a meth lab, not that I aspired to a Bryan Cranston, *Breaking Bad* role. Walking in, I was pleasantly surprised to find a fully equipped machine shop with two ultralight planes and one homemade airplane. I immediately pictured myself passing on aviation lore and knowledge in a "Why yes, I fly jets" cocky kind of way.

Rather than cockiness, a more apt description is quietly self-assured, especially if I compared myself to some of my classmates at school who had way more reason to be cocky than I do. I was content with how my career had gone but disappointed with what appeared to be that career's end. This first career ending was definitely not storybook. In comparison to those I went to the Air Force Academy with, one roommate had been a space-shuttle pilot selectee until the Challenger accident, the guy across the hall from me was a veteran shuttle pilot of three space missions, and the others were an even number of fighter, bomber, tanker, and transport pilots who were in my squadron back then. Heck, even Captain Sully of USAir "Miracle on the Hudson" was a year ahead of my class, staying not too far away in the next dorm. It is easier to be humble when you compare yourself to the caliber of people around you. I mentioned earlier about being the sum total of the five people you hang with the most. Well, if you want to be more successful, make sure those five people are living at a higher caliber than you. Those guys in my Air Force Academy certainly set the bar high for me.

At near fifty-seven years of age, I wondered if this aviation school was my new calling. I quietly affirmed to myself that I could mentor these students; I could make a difference at this school given a chance. Walking in, I was greeted by the lead teacher, and we struck up a great conversation. Yes, he could use me for part or all of the school day, even though I knew my availability was closer to 24/7/365, family duties exempted. He described the student population as "at-risk," but he assured me I would not have to deal with the discipline side. The lead teacher described the curriculum as teaching students about machine safety, OSHA rules, first-aid, and fundamental life skills for the trades or factory assembly lines, as well as the basic high-school core subjects. We shook hands, and I started the following Wednesday, even before I completed any paperwork or background checks. It is always speedier when you are remotely located from the administration … or is it that they feel the need to put their stamp by necessity?

Run by the public-school district, I found the program a satisfying challenge and learned a lot. We spent a lot of time teaching basic shop and tool skills, emphasizing safety and standard practices. We actually used the two ultralight airplanes as labs. As stated, the down side was that the school was essentially a convenient place for the district to place their "at-risk" students, but what an opportunity to learn how to deal with teenage students! I soaked up everything I could and actually learned more than I taught, especially from the lead teacher. The biggest takeaway was to allow the student to fix his/her own behavior by asking four questions:

- What are you doing?
- What are you supposed to be doing?
- Are you doing it?
- What are you going to do about it?

What a way to maintain control without making the students feel admonished or manipulated. Genius, huh? It was probably something from one of those academic books taught during school professional-development days, but I like to think the genius was in the lead teacher's unique application.

The school's emphasis was introducing these "at risk" students to career technical education courses. Not all students can or should look for college degrees, particularly considering the college debt one usually accumulates. Yet the direction public education has gone, pushing all students toward college degrees, seems the primary focus for school curriculums. Research actually shows shortages in the trades and technical jobs ... so much so that many of the trade jobs can bring six-figure incomes within five to ten years.

Frustration has a way of creeping in when dealing with students, especially with those "at risk." Why do we call them "at risk" anyway? My first answer was because this student population was behind in every category of learning, as well as social/life skills. Long discussions with the lead teacher and observations of how he and the staff dealt with these students revealed a better answer. Broken homes, drugs, and gangs are all factors, but what really stuck out was the fact that there was no one for them to rely on, no structure, no support system, and no accountability. Over half the class of thirty-two students, if they showed up for class, partook of the free breakfast we offered, and often times left within minutes of eating, being more engaged with their friends (often time gang members) who provided some sense of belonging. One time, I lamented to the lead teacher out loud, asking what we were really accomplishing. With a sagacious wink, he said, "You'll see. One of these times, you will catch a glimpse of a spark in one of the students and say, 'Oh, that's it! He or she gets what we are trying to do.'"

We introduced some subtle incentives for arriving on time and staying for the duration of classes. The lead teacher suggested custom uniforms with name patches, a school-logo patch, and country-of-origin flags sewn onto the sleeves in exchange for arriving on time with consistency and staying to the end of the school day. I spent the considerable part of two days asking local uniform stores for donations and found a company who graciously agreed to donate fifty dark blue workshop coveralls in various sizes. With a limited budget, we had the students list their name, graduation year, and country of origin. We handed out the uniforms, based on an attendance formula, and suddenly we had nearly thirty students arriving on time and staying for the duration, but we still had some slackers to work on.

Their gratification in their uniforms was evident. The countries of origin ranged from Ethiopia, Somalia, and Guatemala to Mexico and Poland. The name patches became sources of pride, and students began self-policing safety violations in the shop area. The uniform incentive was so strong and attendance so vastly improved that we were able to add additional life skills into our daily lessons. After a visit to the Boeing assembly line, we introduced similar reporting/attendance procedures as the Boeing teams. We even organized the group into daily roll-call flights of ten students each, where the senior-most student could report absences in their flight during our morning roll call. I still hadn't seen the spark the lead teacher alluded to earlier, but this was a step in the right direction.

The spark came in due time but not before experiencing more frustration and actually quite comical situations. The first one occurred one day as I opened the garage-door entrance to the shop and found three boys huddled around a smoking apple, from which issued the pungent smell of weed. In my best Marine gunny-sergeant voice, I bellowed, "What are you doing?" Entertaining sheepish smiles all around, they tossed the apple into the trash, which I easily retrieved. I guess the apple-core technique gets used when Zig-Zag paper is not available, and I think, comes from the movie, *Bill and Ted's Excellent Adventure*. Who says movies don't teach us anything or influence kids?

I directed them inside to the lead teacher's office, presenting the apple evidence and relating what had happened. The lead teacher immediately picked up the phone, and in the ensuing conversation, I realized we were all completely out of any discussion or investigation. The school district counselors would handle everything from here forward, ranging from the investigation to the discipline and counseling.

Here is the funny part: The conversation drifted from English to Spanish, with all participating in the investigation. I got the general drift of the investigation but not all of it, since my Spanish is limited to useful phrases, such as "una mas cervez por favor" or "donde esta la biblioteca?" Once we got to the discipline part, entirely in Spanish, I realized the conversation centered on only two of the students. These two were suspended for seven days and could return to school with mandatory weekly drug testing and weekly counseling. Whispering to the lead teacher, I asked about the third student, whom I considered one of the engaged students. The lead teacher explained that this third student would have to go to the county counselors. The school district would not accept him, as this was his third strike.

The last time he left a counseling session, he stole the district's van for a joy ride and ditched it in the middle of one of the suburbs! Comical, but it is a sad tale. According to a police report, during the following summer, this same student was involved in a shooting where he sprayed MAC-10 bullets into the house of a rival gang. It would be interesting to know where he got the gun, but the fact that he was tried as an adult and sentenced to some eight years, even with testimony on his behalf from the lead teacher, is particularly poignant. Sadly, the teacher told me the sentencing results, and you could see the lost look his eyes as he told me that this eighteen-year-old would probably be released and become a life-long, hardened criminal.

At the school, we had interesting weekly situations and topics crop up, and occasional disputes resolved; there was never a dull moment. Dealing with fourteen- to eighteen-year-old students with raging hormones can be difficult, and our school was no different. Posturing and disputes periodically erupted into pushing and shoving matches, especially between the boys, many of whom were basically unrepentant grown men.

I inserted myself between two of the grown men one time, wondering all the while, *Mel, what are you thinking?* As the two yelled various four-letter epithets at each other, strutting like gamecocks before a match, I realized it was just for show, with the appearance that I was the sole barrier preventing one or the other from ripping the other's head off. Inside, I had to laugh as I stood between two six-foot bruisers, parading their masculinity.

As other teachers arrived, we somehow extricated the two without resorting to formal disciplinary action. The perfect description comes from the Japanese word *tatemae,* or the act of saving face in public—or in this case, in front of their peers. Situation defused, the two gamecocks eventually settled back into the routine. I think maybe the current PC climate would have required mandatory counseling, statements in their permanent record, and the like. Remote locations away from administrative red tape and excessive supervision done in the right manner has certain advantages. If only the school administration and parents would just trust trained educators, maybe we would not rely on politically correct solutions to simple disputes.

This brings to mind the Taoist Lao Tzu's quote about the student becoming equal with the master or teacher. "When the student is ready, the teacher will appear. When the student is truly ready, the teacher will disappear." A simple corollary to how the lead teacher handled the situation, tongue-in-cheek: "When the students are truly fighting, the teacher will appear. When the student is truly not fighting, the teacher will disappear." My interpretation of the lead teacher's reaction was that direct intervention was not required and no one was hurt ... practical lesson complete.

Lunch discussions became teaching moments. One conversation was about the need to wait to start a family. The lead teacher asked each of the staff when they got married and when they'd had their first child, and the ages ranged from twenty-nine to thirty-five years old. As we got to the students' parents, the answers ranged from eighteen to twenty-five. I was struck by the dichotomy of perception between family and marriage and the ability to support a family. One of the students with a baby at home was fifteen years old, and his mother was a grandmother at thirty-one! I am not yet a grandpa at sixty-seven. The lesson was that the longer you wait to start a family, the more economically successful you can be. You need to wait to start a family until you establish a career path and have some economic stability. What an eye opener! The cultural divide could not have been more evident. I was still learning more than I was teaching. Who was really the teacher? The students were my sensei. Oh, little grasshopper, you have still much to learn.

Late April came, and as the lead teacher predicted, a glimmer of hope appeared. One of our students was accepted into the local community college's career technical program as a pipe fitter/welder. This success reminded me of Loren Eiseley's story of a beachcomber's early morning beach stroll, when he comes upon thousands of starfish washed up on the shore. In the distance, he sees a small boy carrying starfish back into the water one at a time. He says to the boy, "You know there are thousands of starfish out here."

The boy replies matter of fact, "Yeah, but when the sun gets high, they will die unless I throw them back into the water."

The man replies, "Yeah, but there are thousands, and you won't make a difference."

As he tosses another into the water, the boy says, "It made a difference with that one."

Win this moment, one starfish at a time. The new welding student was a saved starfish; the MAC-10-shooting student seemed to be one the sun got to, but hopefully, in his future, he could be saved by a passing beachcomber.

Previous to and concurrently during this time, through my local school district, I served on six to seven schoolboard committees, including chairing one for placing a $10M bond issue on the next election ballot, which handily passed. One committee was tasked with exploring "alternative school year schedules." The charge was delving into alternatives like year-around school and double day schedules (7:00 a.m.–1:00 p.m., 1:00 p.m.–7:00 p.m.) for more efficient use of school facilities and resources. This alternative-school committee proved interesting, as both internal and external factors provided novel perspectives and opinions.

The ten weeks spent in committee certainly tried all members' patience, as we discussed, cajoled, ranted, and compromised on numerous issues. One night as we brainstormed ideas, I brought up the suggestion of a European-type schedule, which utilizes Saturday for classes. A lady in our group summarily chastised me for the mere mention of Saturdays, as in her religion Saturday is the Sabbath and is inviolable. The very reason we were tasked with finding options for alternative schedules was to explore options. Not only was I chastised but this lady never acknowledged me, addressed me, or looked at me for the final four meetings. How did it come to this? Is there no room for learning or changing our opinions as we glean new data, observations, or perspectives? Besides, Muslim worship is on Fridays, should we factor that? Carol Dweck is credited with the term "growth mindset," and it implies that talent is developed through hard work, good strategies, and a readiness-acceptant feedback, as opposed to the "fixed mindset" that believes talent is innate with no room for improvement. The growth mindset is to learn, recover, and move on, but it is harder when another person does not allow teaching moments to unfold and recovery to take place.

Around this time, I began thinking that, since I wasn't making a lot of progress toward a non-flying aviation job, maybe teaching might be the ticket. While researching Washington State educator school requirements, I found the process cumbersome, lengthy, and costly enough that I would never recover the schooling costs (since I am on a relentless march to "Geezerville"). The Washington State Career Technical Educator program, however, was unique, and allows prospects to complete a career and technical educator (CTE) certificate in less than two years and at a reasonable cost, both online and at community colleges. The cost difference was staggering! Forty to fifty thousand dollars versus ten thousand dollars! I found that that one student's acceptance into the community college career technical program was a truly defining motivational moment. Maybe I could be a Washington State Career Technical Educator.

Career Technical Educators are a welcome addition to schooling, since not all students will attend or aspire to college. The opportunities for high-school graduates to make six-figure salaries in HVAC, plumbing, aviation mechanics, automobile mechanics, electrician trades, etc., is well documented. Also, CTEs have numerous teaching opportunities in STEM (Science, Technology, Engineering, Math)-type courses and aviation-related courses for high school. I completed nine of the twelve courses, but my eye was always toward aviation, and before I could finish, a small window opened. The fact that I did not finish still weighs on me, because I feel I may have let the lead teacher down. If you're reading this, sir, remember this: "It's not the actual help we receive to fix something. It's the thought that someone else thought of helping." (Unkown)

While working on the CTE, I still hungered to stay in aviation. Rather than stagnating, I asked myself, "What could make me more versatile, more 'plug and play' as an aviation manager? What would add to my continuous improvement? I know, I'll Google it." Up pops an aviation safety certification course at Embry-Riddle Aeronautical University in Daytona, Florida, for which I more than met all the qualifications and requirements. Three weeks, a hundred and twenty contact hours, and you have the basis for an airline director of flight safety or safety auditor. So off to Daytona I went, attending an excellent course on aviation safety.

I got one tiny reminder while there. I spent a night in the hospital after a heart palpitation episode—scary but not unexpected. Now that I think about it, I wonder if it could it have been my significant other testing my "shock collar…" Nah, no way, that's not like her, and thank goodness, I was out of range.

Back at home after the three weeks, I went back to the grind of applications and continuing the CTE curriculum. This was 2009–2010, and the job market was poor across the board.

The best encouragement came from any company who actually answered my questions or sent a nice "turn-down." I mean, I heard "no" so many times that it reminded me of trying to find a prom date in high school. (Side note: I ended up taking a very beautiful lady to prom, kind of a *Beauty and the Beast* tale.)

8 – LEARN FROM FAILURE

"I've had worries in my life,
most of which never happened."
—Mark Twain

With my new safety credential, fortune smiled during one job-search session: I discovered that my original airline needed a director of flight safety. By hook and by crook, the VP of Safety happened to be one of my classmates from college. I felt I was imminently qualified with my twenty-something years of pilot instruction and eight years as the assistant MD80 fleet captain and MD80 fleet captain, on top of completing the flying safety certification course at Embry-Riddle University.

Sometimes, the best laid plans fall through, and while I initially had a verbal agreement from the VP to work as the director of flight safety, it fell through the cracks. The offer came while I was on vacation, and I wanted to immediately return home and sign all the paperwork, but the VP told me to finish my three-week vacation. In those three weeks, the VP was asked to resign, and the "verbal offer" evaporated, with not even an email exchange to verify an offer.

I had faith the new VP would at least interview me, but no dice; I was bypassed. The way I see it, you have successes and you have learning events, but never failures. This was a hard pill to swallow, so close to returning somewhere I had been a part of for twenty-eight years. "There are no secrets to success. It is the result of preparation, hard work, and learning from failure," Colin Powell once said. I went back to the drawing board—back to square one. The Japanese proverb, *"Nana korobi, ya oki"* comes to mind, which means, "Fall down seven times, get up eight."

I assumed there was a lot of back-channel brokering going on between HR, legal, and the out-going/incoming Safety VPs. The CEO invited me to his office for a chat with the express purpose of discussing the politics behind the director of flight safety position. As the discussion developed, I realized his concern was either that I might protest or sue over the verbal agreement or that there was some background conflict. Maybe I had cause for suit, but there was no way I would go down that path. This company had been my home for over twenty-eight years, and to this day, I still bleed blue (the company logo color). Besides, I could deal with it, and there had to be alternatives, right?

So now what? Where was God leading me now? I had always promised my wife we would move back to her roots in the Chicago area when the opportunity came. I mean, all the "outlaws" and relatives lived within an hour or so, so why couldn't I remake myself with an aviation job in the Chicago area?

After hundreds of completed applications, an opportunity arose while researching one aviation company's online posts, finding the name of the vice president of operations, and guessing at his email address. I sent off a personalized email with my tailored resume and received an offer for an interview. The interview was mostly us talking about experiences and common friends and getting a tour of the flight operations area. In retrospect, there sure were a lot of empty cubicles and a heavy undertone of "we really need someone to fill this position." The euphoria of finding an aviation job near Chicago may have clouded my reasoning, because it appeared to check all the boxes, and I ignored the flags.

The near six-figure offer came within three days, and I became a manager of flight standards for an international, non-schedule carrier about one-hour northwest of Chicago in Rockford. As a matter of fact, this carrier, now defunct, had six Boeing 767s, one Boeing 757, and fifteen McDonnell-Douglas MD80s. The MD80s, by coincidence, were the same airplanes I flew at my original carrier for twenty-seven years. The MD80s were sub-leased to the U.S. Marshall Service, whose job was sending undocumented (illegal) workers back to their countries of origin, so the U. S. Marshalls flew into unique airfields like Guantanamo, Cuba, a refueling stopover, and Tegucigalpa Airport in Honduras.

Some of the flights were flown by company pilots too, rather than U.S. Marshalls. Despite the political ramifications, the uniqueness and dangerous airport aspects provided plenty of challenges. The other challenges dealt with the distinct require-ments of flying two-engine airliners overwater, under the FAA guidelines of extended-range twin-engine operational-perfor-mance standards, or ETOPS. Most people have little knowl-edge of overwater operations rules, which are quite extensive. Tongue in cheek, we referred to it as "**E**ngines **T**urn **O**r **P**eople **S**wim" operations. What a way to quench my desire to remain working in aviation.

I was able to work with some great people, but I always felt everyone was hunkered down in their cubicle bunkers—the notorious "silo" mentality. New jobs mean developing new relationships, and working relationships take a while to develop. The airline had begun a number of years earlier and had a familial feel. The longtime employees still had a sense of camaraderie, much like at my previous one, but had since fallen on hard times and had been bought out by a real-estate company. I resolved to be like a coffee bean in water, permeating those around me with some positivity, one person at a time, trying to change plain water into gourmet coffee.

The original company employees had a strong bond, and the airline's trials and tribulations caused a protective "circle the wagons" mentality, which was hard to penetrate. As the newest arrival, my acceptance took a while, but my gregarious nature helped. I even started a Friday "lunch bunch," which started a communication, connection, commitment, and caring cycle where we alternated choosing lunch spots around the city of Rockford, IL. (Side note: Rockford is the fifth largest city in Illinois. Cliffy from the sitcom *Cheers* would love the trivia.)

We actually rotated between some six to eight diners at one time. We had great conversations, creating the business relationships necessary for trust and genuine friendships. I may have provided the initial impetus, but the idea flourished with the company's director of safety.

Unfortunately, sometimes the best of intentions are overcome by events outside an employee's control. The reality was that the real-estate company that owned the airline had not been doing well since the Great Recession of 2008–2009, and definitely had no background in sustaining a 24/7/365 worldwide operation like an airline. Talk about opposites. Real estate was an open market, "dog eat dog," one-upmanship, art of the deal with few rules (except make as much as you can) industry. While it exhibits a similarly competitive, money-making goal, the airline industry is a highly regulated, standardized, no safety compromises, no short-cuts-allowed industry, and conflicts between the real-estate owners and the senior airline executives routinely occurred. Uncompromising and arrogant to a fault, the owners routinely overrode those with endlessly better qualifications and experience—the airline's veteran employees—which was a disaster looking for a place to happen.

When it came time to add a new jumbo jet to the fleet, the real-estate side tried to step in with their "real-estate negotiating," finding large, three-hundred-plus seating aircraft, like an Airbus 330, from India or an Egyptian Boeing 777. The thinking seemed to be, "We buy large land parcels and large shopping malls for millions. It is not a quantum leap to buy used, surplus aircraft for millions." Unfortunately, the process is not as simple as walking onto the airplane lot, picking one with a pretty color, and flying off. The process is long and tedious, with months of back and forth, including a review of maintenance records from the airplane's inception, crew retraining, the consideration of unique tools and equipment, qualifications, and (needless to say) some countries do not enforce aviation standards to the extent the FAA does. The bottom line is that the real-estate "negotiators" did not deal well with the rigors of the FAA oversight, and bulldog tactics did not help.

The new aircraft searches were moot anyway. I began seeing cracks in the airline's foundation, starting with how the real-estate company was bleeding the airline's revenue after all the real-estate holdings in 2010 were in the tank. The airline was a convenient revenue stream propping the real-estate holdings up. Still, the passion and pride within my fellow airline employees was apparent. Unfortunately, all the hard work they put in to bring either a Boeing 777 or an Airbus 330 to compliment the Boeing 767 workhorses appeared to be for naught. We finally had the FAA onboard with approval on each preliminary step, but the financial side (read: "real-estate company") shall we say, fell short in numerous ways. The financing was not there.

Non-scheduled airlines are notorious for working on a shoestring budget, and the writing was on the wall with the inability to finance either the B777 or A330. The airline was edging toward bankruptcy. The demise was inevitable. The real-estate owners had bled too much equity from the airline and evidently missed too many deadlines. The deadline would pass without an offer or counter offer on the wide-body airplanes. In fact, the passing deadlines reminded me of a Douglas Adams quote: "I love deadlines. I like the whooshing sound they make as they fly by." The deadlines were definitely whooshing and no deal was consummated.

Health wise, I continued to do well. After moving to Illinois, I developed a great relationship with my new cardiologist, even though he is a White Sox fan. (What self-respecting Chicago north-sider could stoop to being a White Sox fan? Yuk!) We had a lot of common ground, since he had also gone to college chasing his dream to become a pilot. During his training, certain realizations became discouraging, however, such as the low starting pay, the time away from home, and the length of time it would take to be hired to a major airline in order to make the "big bucks." So he'd switched to chasing medical school. Speaking with him now, it's clear that he is *way too smart* to be a pilot, and that's why he became a cardiologist. I am fortunate to have him as my cardiologist, and from the first time we met, we kindled a special relationship.

We also agreed I would use him as my primary-care physician. He even gave me his personal cellphone number to call if I ever needed. I occasionally use it but took care to think about the circumstances. However, though he is brilliant helping me take care of my body, I am not sure he could qualify to help me mentally, at least not judging by his choice of favorite baseball team.

Anyway, my cardiac/primary-care physician is on my superhero list, and the staff he has working for him is outstanding. I built strong relationships with them and can contact them any time for prescription renewals, referrals, or just for answers to any medical question. I try to thank them all after every visit with a Starbucks card or goodie bag of some sort. I mean, if we worked together, we would probably meet up for happy hour, so what difference does it make if it's coffee or a margarita anyway? People remember you for the little gratitude-filled things you do, which build relationships.

In 2012, I had a series of episodes of lightheadedness and dizziness, and various symptoms similar to a heart attack but never any actual occurrences. I had another heart-vein issue, appearing constricted in a few tests, but up to that point, the risk of placing another stent in my heart had always been deemed riskier than leaving the vein as it was. With the lightheadedness, though, my doctor changed his recommendation and another stent placement became necessary.

The lightheadedness was a concerning symptom, indicating an increased likelihood of another heart attack. It's amazing how in-tune you get with your body after you have an epiphany-type health issue. (Side note: Other than this incident in 2012, my three- to four times-per-week exercise regimen continues to keep me healthy. Like I said previously, the regimen is not an "Iron Man, beach body" routine, but staying active has made a difference.)

This stent placement, like the first one, was a serious surgery, but it can be almost routine to a highly qualified cardiologist like mine. The short hospital stay makes the procedure seem like an outpatient surgery, since I was barely in the hospital two and a half days. On the positive side, I got to eat the fine hospital haute cuisine. Did you notice? I used my new perspective: positive thoughts, positive spin. Changing my perspective from "I have to eat the hospital food" to "I get to eat hospital food." You see the philosophical difference? No? Me neither. It's still hospital food, Mellen. But staying positive *is* very important to your health and well-being. I did feel obligated to ask the day nurse if she could send an agent to the room so we could talk about a timeshare, since I was there for over two days and might need to return someday. I think I got a snicker.

The job security seemed to be ebbing. The airline kept grasping at straws, trying to stay alive, managing as long as we did in no small part due to the original employees' efforts to keep it afloat. Unfortunately, the real-estate leadership was bleeding the airline like an eighteenth-century doctor bloodletting his patients. The time came to reset and start the "Indeed, Glassdoor, and LinkedIn" sequence again. This time, I landed a job fairly quickly as the head of pilot training with a regional carrier flying fifty-seat regional jet aircraft on the east coast, but based in nearby Wisconsin. Great job, great people; however, due to the innate airline uncertainty and my youngest son starting high school, Heidi and I decided not to move. So, I commuted to Wisconsin on Monday mornings, stayed in an apartment, and returned home on Fridays. The weekly absence was not a recipe for success, but I was not giving up on my aviation purpose—not yet anyway.

Loneliness for both myself and Heidi was probably a natural reaction. I would return on Fridays, and we did not have much time together that evening. Saturday was our date night, where we tried to catch up on everything. My absence created some resentment, but we endeavored to make the best of it. One Saturday dinner, after half a bottle of wine, I pensively leaned into the table and asked, "Heidi, am I the only one?"

To which she answered, "Well, I dated quite a few eights and one or two sevens, but yeah, you're the only one." I wish I could take credit for that joke, and I've long since forgotten who to give the credit to, but it is great to be the only "one" in someone's eyes.

As the head of pilot training for near six hundred pilots, about twenty instructors, and five different pilot bases, I became acutely aware of the supervisory problems the locations caused.

One rumor had it that instructors at several pilot bases were short-circuiting the FAA time and curriculum requirements for recurrent training and needed more supervision. I made it a point to attend the training at all locations on a periodic basis. It was easy for me to travel, because whether I stayed at my apartment near the headquarters or in a hotel on the road, it made no difference.

The supervisory visits re-emphasized the importance of maintaining standards. Ohio State's legendary coach Urban Meyer stresses fewer rules and more of an adherence to a standard of conduct. His refrain is "you are either above the line or below the line on our standards," and it yields a standard language and tone for your team's culture. Aviation has so many rules and regulations. Some are in conflict with others, and no one could possibly remember them all, so an overall standard certainly helps. I felt that visiting all the sites periodically was important to maintaining standards and certainly helped me communicate with the remote bases. I wanted to engrain a feeling of staying above the line. I was trying to be the coffee bean that transforms plain water into gourmet coffee one instructor, one pilot, one employee at a time. Not an impossible task, but I needed help and stepped on some toes, even though my intentions were good.

I tried to bring more supervision to the evaluator pilots too, by proposing they be put under the pilot training department. Placing the evaluators separately under the training department, alongside the instructor pilots, made sense from a standardization point of view, but my boss felt differently. In true military fashion of "lead, follow, and get the hell out of the way," I looked for options. One good work-around was monthly communication via conference calls, Zoom-type calls, and/or GoToMeeting exchanges. The evaluators picked up on the importance of these conversations for maintaining standards between the simulator pilots, instructor pilots, and evaluators. The uptick in communications started to bridge the trust gap. Communications builds relationships, which leads to trust and caring. This was a start on a work-around.

I struggled with connecting with my boss, the VP of Flight Operations. At thirty-eight years old, he and I had a significant difference in age and background. My background was Air Force and a major airline, and his was crop-duster, law degree, and regional carrier. On one of my supervisory trips, the VP came along for a Gemba Walk. A Japanese business concept, *Gemba* literally translates to "the actual/real place" and is defined as the importance of leadership understanding what is happening at every company level. For this visit, we went to three different bases. I thought it was a great idea, and that maybe I could work on building a better relationship with my boss. Trust begins with communication and what better way than spending a few days chatting with the boss over meals and adult beverages?

My wife said I should tell him my "Bluebird Day" story, complete with my health drama, because it might help us connect better. After all, relationships within teams was my bailiwick (I felt) and revealing yourself, exposing your vulnerabilities, can help connect with others. Over beers and appetizers one night on the trip, I related my story and believed he listened with rapt attention.

In retrospect, I was naïve in thinking I had connected with him somehow. Two days into the trip, the VP returned to headquarters, and I continued to visit two other bases. The next day, I called to update him on a couple of pending issues, but when I began, he interrupted me, saying that he needed to see me in person as soon as I returned the next day. I naively thought he had urgent business to attend to and needed off the call.

Returning the next day, I went straight to his office, where an acquaintance from HR was present. The gist of it was that I was being terminated, and since I was an "at will" employee, no reason was given. I tried numerous ways of asking but got the same answer each time. On this matter, there would be no closure. I asked if there was an option to resign, and they said yes, that would be okay. I also asked if there was any compensation or ways to pay off the remaining five months of my apartment lease and how it affected my pay. The HR person had all the answers: Yes, the apartment was covered, and there was a severance package of several months' pay, continued medical coverage, blah, blah, blah. Then I was told I needed to clear out my office immediately, take some paperwork (to be signed within a week), and be escorted out of the building. Stunned, I said, "I'm not sure why, but I can assure you I will leave with dignity and my integrity intact. I'll let you know about the paperwork." I will not write what I really wanted to say. I misjudged the level of confidentiality and trust I could or should expect from a working-relationship perspective. Valiant effort, tough lesson, but in the end, I was better off, and I would be at home.

I drove immediately home, some three hours away. I would sort out the apartment and furniture over the weekend. Driving home, I went over and over the details, trying to figure out where I had gone wrong or what I had done wrong. My performance review had been pretty good, and other than normal conflicts over day-to-day operations, I could not think where we had gone sideways. At my previous airline, conflicting opinions were encouraged, but once the decision trigger was pulled, we set about executing it. I was knee-deep in the transition to an FAA mandated flight-training change to Advanced Qualification Program (AQP) and had several other ideas turned down, but nowhere could I see where we worked at cross purposes. My boss and I seemed to get along okay, but our philosophies differed, as I preferred to rehabilitate rather than fire and he had a different take. In my opinion, his was a good example of a boss rather than a servant leader. The one proposition I was persistent on was getting a pay raise for the manager of AQP, because his pay was grossly out of whack when compared to the same position at other regional carriers (by a factor of 25 percent).

Halfway back home, I thought of the "Bluebird Day" story and the possibility that the VP might think I would cost the company medical or life-insurance money. No sour grapes, but I had already considered leaving, once the training department finished the on-going AQP project I was deeply committed to finishing. Living away from home five days a week was too big a price to pay for any length of time, and I had been going at it for over eight months. In the ensuing months, I found out that the company never refilled my position, and the manager of AQP happily received a significant pay raise. Since my position was not refilled, I can guess where the money came from for the manager's pay raise, and the company still saved money.

Nonetheless, the termination was a tough pill to swallow, but what goes around comes around. A few years later, this VP was set to interview for the VP of flight operations at my original airline, and several of my peers contacted me for my opinion. I gave them my opinion, and told them I could do one better, since I still had contact with that airline's CEO, whom I had volunteered with on a couple of schoolboard committees some years back. I sent my original airline's CEO a formal email, relaying in a polite manner that the VP candidate was not of the same leadership ilk as the culture mandated and would not fit the airline's management style, though if the company needed a boss, he would fit the bill. To his credit, the CEO answered the email within a day and thanked me for the input, telling me he valued my opinion. What's good for the goose is good for the gander. The airline did not hire the VP, probably due to a better-qualified internal candidate, but I still felt I had an input.

The Wisconsin job had been challenging in many respects, but the absence from home for five days a week had been a very interesting challenge. Check that—it was extremely burdensome and led to conflicts at home. Bluntly, I was selfishly thinking more of ambition and tried to bury the reality of how Heidi felt, handling almost everything at home on her own. The biggest issue resting on her lone shoulders, which I avoided confronting and selfishly kept compartmentalized, was that my high-school son had Crohn's Disease and was routinely missing school. He missed at least one day a week, and this did not include occasionally missing more due to side effects from either drugs or infusions as the doctors struggled for an answer to controlling his Crohn's. He finally underwent surgery, removing a sizable portion of his intestines, and found significant improvement from the combined surgery and anti-inflammatory drugs. He recovered quickly and actually started regaining a healthy amount of weight for his size and age.

I am skimming over a lot of the details, but he is one tough kid, who took several lessons to heart from his affliction. The main lesson was empathy for others afflicted with chronic diseases. Another was the discovery of his persistence and drive. Arguably a very good baseball player, my son and I spent countless hours practicing with hitting lessons and father-son cage sessions. Tryouts for the high-school baseball team were disappointing, as he was let go with the last cut, but to his credit, he took it in stride. Today, he claims that some of the baseball lessons inspired him through college and his acceptance into an MBA program at the University of Wisconsin—Madison.

Persistence, grit, and "what's important next" (W.I.N.) are deeply ingrained in his mind.

This is not to say my other three sons do not have persistence and grit too. Each in their own way has faced or are facing their own adversities. I am constantly in awe of their talent and hard work. The career routes they have taken present great opportunities in cinematography. The oldest does freelance films and is a professor at a university, the second oldest does films and works with advertising, and the third is a movie sound designer and musician. Cinematography and music are definitely fields where you need persistence in the face of barrages of rejections.

Another lesson that was for all my sons (and me) is that none of us communicate much about problems. What is it about men not wanting to speak, much less speak freely? Is it not manly to show feelings? Somehow, men are raised to believe they need to handle things solo, remain reticent, and not divulge their feelings. Men, typically, need solitude to brood and figure things out. However, those men who finally figure it out—those men who realize how a friendship or a spousal relationship can become more meaningful through better communication—find more happiness.

Brené Brown states it succinctly: "Building better relationships by revealing your vulnerability builds trust and communications." It is the key to successful teams. During my time away, we (Heidi and I) lost our close communication link, so our relationship drifted a bit. If I could not see the crux of the problem, divine intervention would fix it for me. Anyway, ninety-eight percent of our conflicts during the Crohn's and Wisconsin time periods were a result of my non-communication. Bottom line, the Wisconsin job was not the best in terms of that, so leaving the job after eight months was a good thing for us. *It is said we have successes but never failures, only lessons learned." Innately stubborn, I learned yet another lesson the hard ward way.*

A job that "gives meaning and purpose" was (and is) elusive, especially when I compare them to my career airline. I held two different airline jobs in a three-year period and neither sufficed. They say that, to climb a wall, you need a ladder, and must take one ladder rung at a time. What if I had the ladder on the wrong wall? I was not very open-minded about a career do-over. After all, my career goal from ten years of age had a singleness in purpose: being a pilot. In retrospect, I can see why I had blinders on for other opportunities. It was time to remake myself—again.

Now what? What's next? The International Airline Transport Association, based in Canada, is the association that maintains the agreements and safety standards for nearly all airlines worldwide. Through courses and certifications, I was able to secure a job as a safety auditor and worked as a consultant for a company who provided instructor-pilot classes under contract to numerous international carriers. I provided initial aircraft-instructor tools and personal, practical lesson experiences on how to utilize the tools.

On numerous occasions, I traveled to Kenya, the Philippines, Cape Verde, and various other places, either conducting the instructor-pilot classes or doing safety audits. The instructor classes were the best forum yet for delving into my experiences and finding practical applications for instructors in the latest crew-resource-management techniques of communication, workload management, leadership, decision-making, and flight discipline. I reveled in it, from start to finish. These were four-and-a-half-day courses and very well received. The pay was lucrative, in that I could earn as much as a month's pay, at the non-scheduled and regional carriers, in a matter of those four and a half days. An added benefit was the freedom

I had to design the course from start to finish, using almost all of the media available. I created original presentations supplemented with various other curriculum segments, which I was intimately familiar with from my previous airline employers.

The safety audits were also a good challenge. The 290 air carriers world-wide belong to the International Air Transportation Association (IATA) based in Montreal, Canada. Similar to the business ISO 9000 audits, IATA has eight certified and designated auditing firms, called IOSA auditors, to maintain a standard of safety that all have agreed to follow. In the manner of the old Ohio State football Coach Urban Meyer, the audit basically stipulates a member airline is "above the line and below the line" of the agreed standards. Below-the-line standards would prohibit operations in and out of member countries until corrected.

Exciting stuff, but it became too exciting when I was scheduled to return to Nairobi, Kenya after a terrorist attack, which killed over seventy people, occurred some three miles from our hotel. I turned down the next opportunity and was never asked back. Unfortunate, but I did not want my wife to worry more than she already did with my heart condition and being half a world away. Besides, she needed better heart "shock collar" range. (The ICD remote's range is not unlimited, so there was no telling how much trouble I could cause that far away from home.)

I was still in search of validation and relevancy. So, I thought, *Now what?* I thought of professional speaking. After all, to paraphrase Liam Nielsen from the movie *Taken*, "I may have few skills, but what I do have are some unique speaking skills, which make me a nightmare for my mom and wife." The excitement of engaging an audience is an adrenaline rush. I set a goal to be a mentor, coach, and/or mental-performance guru, often asked to speak at conferences.

The question became, "How do I gain the expertise and name recognition to be a paid speaker?" I stumbled on Brian Cain and Ken Ravizza, both athletic mental-performance gurus. *Hey, this is good stuff for coaching!* Reading and listening to audio books on mental performance became an absolute obsession. I finished the Brian Cain Mental Performance Master certification. Man, it was good stuff—stuff I could mentor with, stuff I could make a difference with, and maybe ... I could eventually coach sports too! Gladwell, Covey, Goggins, Willink, Duckworth, Afremow, and Davis. Wow! I ate that stuff up. Coyle, Dweck, Ehrmann, Krzyzewski, Dungy, Sinek, Brown, and all of the new and innovative coaching superstars ... the list goes on and on. Podcasts, webinars and conferences blurred into one dynamo of purpose. The one writer who sticks in my mind most is Jon Gordon, author of *The Energy Bus*, *Power of Positive Leadership,* and his whole coaching, leading, and self-help series. I could make a difference with this stuff!

Concurrently, I happened upon a couple of high-school-baseball coaching jobs. I like baseball, and I'd coached eight- to seventeen-year-olds for some twenty years with my sons and by myself. Granted, this was on a different competitive level, but those coaches really imprint on their players like a baby robin imprinting on the first thing they see after birth. These coaches leave their stamp on players for life. I call it the thirty-year plan. In thirty years, these coaches will embody the little voice in the players' heads, whispering encouragement, mottos, and sayings that will help them deal with success, loss, and failure in a transformational way. *Anyway,* I figured, *what have I got to lose?* I tried to figure out what it would take to be considered.

At the same time, my search happened upon franchise opportunities. I interviewed with two different franchises and seemed to do fairly well, with both offering me opportunities to continue with the onboarding process. At some point in the process, I finally asked Heidi her opinion, and contrary to previous forays and searches, it was all a welcome change, according to Heidi. Without "phoning a friend," or "asking the audience," I listened to her and eventually agreed on one thing: The franchise was not a good idea, so I dropped the idea as impractically expensive and too much stress.

Back to the coaching idea. Providence provided an opportunity. The Illinois High School Baseball Association or associated sources have several certification courses. I thought, *Why not take them and see where the cards fall? Besides, at least I won't have to get on the Indeed, Glassdoor, or LinkedIn carousel again.* I earned the certifications, applied to several staffs, and lo and behold, the high school up the street from me asked me to interview.

A six-on-one interview would be intimidating to even a seasoned interview veteran. I had previously sent my complete two-page resume, which I was reluctant to show because I figured most of the resume dealt with leadership and business positions over coaching skills. The panel, however, was intrigued enough to ask pertinent questions. After all, I was not a threat as a non-pay volunteer. The interview was cordial, and later, I found out that my answers to a couple of questions put me over the top. Specifically, the answer to whether I would be able to be an assistant caught their attention. I had answered with a short message to the effect of "lead, follow, or get the h*ll out of the way." The school could not offer a paid position, but I was welcome to volunteer. *The head coach, who has coached over 25 years, may have gambled on me, but with all his experience he says he recognized I could make a difference.* (Thanks Coach "Murrdog", not his real name.)

Coaching baseball at the high-school level would be a uniquely challenging experience I'd never had before, so I knew I needed to open up and be alert for learning opportunities.

When going into a new or threatening environment, the Air Force has a process called the OODA loop. The acronym was invented by an Air Force fighter pilot named Colonel John Boyd, who applied the loop process to combat operations. Essentially, the concept is a process cycle to quickly observe and react to events more rapidly than normal, and has applicability to business and sports. The cycle teaches to observe, orient, decide, and act. For contemplation, compare it to the Shewhart Cycle of plan-do-check-act. Anyway, it was time to re-orient again, time to remake, and time for a second chance.

I certainly went through the OODA cycle while finding coaching, and continued to use it in my new challenge: coaching baseball at the high-school level. Lucky for me, I had a great mentor in the freshman coach I was assigned to assist. I began calling him *Sensei*, after all, he been coaching and teaching high schoolers for nearly thirty years. He set the example for maintaining a calm demeanor and enjoying the moment without raising your anxiety level. Some of his mound visits were classics, including one where all the players on the field came in, expecting a pitching replacement, and all I heard was something like, "Is this fun? Let's just play some baseball here." Every element of observe, orient, decide, and act in a simple sentence.

9 – FIGHTING GEEZERVILLE

"He will win who knows when to fight
and when not to fight."
—Sun Tzu

I coached my first spring as a volunteer baseball coach. As exciting as it was, in the back of my mind, I knew aviation was still my true love. Coaching serious baseball was always on my bucket list, but I still wanted to re-capture the "if you love your job, you'll never work a day of your life" feeling. Besides, I had too much time on my hands during the seven-month "off-season." The daily humdrum of my off-season routine—yardwork, bills, and workouts—was hard to process. *Is this it? Am I resigned to this? Is the off-season meant to ease the transition to "Geezerville?"*

One day, I succumbed to a thought: "Maybe I should just take a peek at some of these LinkedIn aviation jobs." BAM! Up pops an opening at a major airline based in New York, one in which I fit the requirements to a "T." Should I go for it? If for no other reason than just to see what the offer might be? I secured an interview for the role of director of flight safety and flew to New York. Questions skipped through my head. Was this an ego thing? Had I learned nothing from the Wisconsin venture?

The interview went very well, and we had numerous connections—people we all knew intimately—so I knew personal recommendations could push me over the top. I made follow-up calls, emails, and HR contacts over the following month or so but never received an indication of when the decision might be made. I finally did the right thing and removed myself from consideration. I decided that it was not in my family's or my own best interest, for sure. It was an epiphany. Eureka! I finally resolved to concentrate on the important people, stop worrying about myself, and tackle the goal of becoming a great coach in my own backyard.

There is a scene in *The Last Samurai* where Tom Cruise's character, Nathan Algren, after hours of arduous training with the simulated bamboo-stock swords, challenges Ujio, Katsumoto's fierce right-hand man. Ujio is a ferocious warrior and knocks Algren down several times. A somewhat sympathetic Nobutada has this advice for Algren:

Nobutada says, "Please forgive. Too many mind."

Algren: "Too many mind?"

Nobutada: "Hai. Mind the sword, mind the people watch, mind the enemy, too many mind…. No mind."

Algren realizes this is good advice, refocuses, and visualizes Ujio's sequence of parries and thrusts. This results in a draw. Though fictional, the lesson this offers is that, when confronted with multiple stresses and threats, switch from "too many mind" to "no mind." Persistence. Grit. Deal with it. So, if I was to be a complete and impactful baseball coach, I had to rid myself of "too many mind" and concentrate on the task at hand.

"What an opportunity I have!" I said to myself. "I should bury myself in baseball. Coaching, motivating, leading—all are right in my wheelhouse." For over four years, I had searched for validation, challenge, and opportunity, and there it was, right up the street from me. I will always be grateful to Coach "Murrdog" for giving me the opportunity. I knew I could fit in, but the question was how long it would take to belong, because there is a big difference between thinking you fit in and actually doing so. Belonging means acceptance as a knowledgeable and capable peer. Belonging means you can expose your vulnerability without rejection or exposure. It means your input is important, and others can consider it in their decisions. I am not sure how long it took to belong, but it was not instantaneous. Besides, being vulnerable in "man vernacular" is normally frowned upon, as it may indicate that you're not independent—a degree of the worst trait possible—a "wussy," or any similar epitaph, especially in the world of raging, testosterone-fueled baseball. Anyway, after an appropriate time, I belonged.

Coaching became an all-consuming passion. However, finding my role was difficult. I did not have the NCAA Division I experience and never will. For the longest time, I was somewhat intimidated by the experience some of the coaches had, but I realized that 80 percent of quality coaching comes from years of coaching experience and not the NCAA playing time. The other 20 percent would always be an edge, so I would do what I could. I did find books, attended conferences, and studied other coaches, all the while figuring I would find my niche, my role, and try to become indispensable. There are rare examples of MLB managers who never played in the "BIGS." Buck Showalter and Earl Weaver come to mind. The point is that there is no replacement for the 20 percent NCAA or MLB playing experience, but with hard work, study, and experience, the possibility of becoming a "respectable coach" exists. My goal remains to be an excellent, go-to coach along the lines of those Illinois High School Baseball Coach Association Hall of Fame inductees. Why settle for ordinary?

Vince Lombardi once said, "Gentlemen, we will chase perfection, and we will chase it relentlessly, knowing all the while we can never attain it. But along the way, we shall catch excellence." If my goal is to mentor, make a difference, and serve, then chasing perfection synchronizes perfectly.

Despite figures from a book called *The Outliers* by Malcolm Gladwell, I sincerely hoped it would not take ten years or ten thousand hours to master coaching. No shortcuts exist, but relentless pursuit of perfection is a worthy goal. Besides, Earl Weaver with the Orioles won a pennant in his first full year as manager. Maybe the stars aligned, and he had the right people on the bus that first year, so there is hope. Take care of the next two hundred feet, or in baseball parlance, the next ninety feet, and you will eventually reach your goal.

In the pursuit, as Coach "Murrdog" is primed to say, "Work while you wait, fill the role we have for you at this time." Resolutely, I accepted any extra duties or assignments from the head coach. The extra duties were definitely in my wheelhouse, considering my organizational abilities. Besides, they say 80 percent of any job is the everyday mundane duties, and 20 percent is the challenging, enjoyable part. In baseball, the best players are not the ones making spectacular web gems but the ones who relentlessly execute the fundamentals over and over again.

Still my impatience cropped up a few times. I desperately wanted recognition as a "good coach," and a "go-to coach" for advice. Advice is not always warranted or wanted, and I occasionally stepped over the bounds of my coaching role and was rightfully put in my place.

Like I stated before, I could never replace the experience of playing college baseball but deeply desired recognition for my twenty-something years of coaching baseball at the ten- to sixteen-year-old range and eight years of high-school coaching. Out of sheer desperation, I made concerted efforts at study, coaching certifications, workshops, and conferences, where I studied coaching principles and mental performance.

Unfortunately, not everyone acknowledges anything short of actual coaching. There is no shortcut to "go-to" coach, and it is a source of frustration even today.

Over the last five years, I am proud to say that I led team fundraising to the tune of over $120,000, with indispensable help from the other coaches, and over $15,000 for cancer research with the crucial help of the team moms. The cancer fundraiser highlighted a particularly poignant story on the actual fundraising day. Prior to the varsity game, the main event, we have a "First Pitch Ceremony" where players with a family member suffering from cancer throw out the first pitch to that family member, usually with between six and ten people participating.

Each year, I unsuccessfully tried to find someone to make a small speech prior to the "First Pitch." No one ever wants to step up, so it devolves to me. I have done a different speech each year, and each time, at some point in the speech, I feel a lump in my throat and a wetness at the corners of my eyes as I choke on the words. It is an emotionally draining experience, and I have yet to make it through a speech. Each "First Pitch" participant is a reminder of my own father's demise at the hands of cancer.

One year, I tried having a few players come up as I said something about the importance of cancer victims having someone to back them up in times of sadness. I had several players designated to pat me on my back gently and say into the microphone, "We got *your* back, coach" as I read off the cancer guests' names to create a sense of caring, but mostly to give me a pause to compose myself. It did not work. Cancer is the enemy, and that "First Pitch Ceremony" for one brief moment, allows the people a small respite in their suffering. The biggest lesson is showing the players something bigger and more important than playing baseball. Seeing their faces during the ceremony is a reward in itself.

These projects, fundraising and such, are not directly related to improving coaching skills, but it is about setting a positive example and honing leadership skills I can transfer to future endeavors. I'm living proof that "work while you wait' is more than a tagline. Remember, the right people on the bus, the wrong people off the bus, and do excellent work in the seat you are assigned, even if your goal is another seat.

10 – NEW BUS RIDERS AND DRIVER

"I'm a school bus driver. What is YOUR Superpower?"
—Author Unknown

The oddity of high-school baseball is that leadership changes every year. Can you visualize the consternation at a company like Ford, Apple, Google, or Campbell's Soup if the top management announced a leadership change, much less an entire C-suite change, every year? High-school teams go through this kind of change nearly every year. New bus driver, new riders, and new seats are part of the yearly transition—the team culture.

One factor in swapping leadership each year is the natural propinquity. (Wow, those S.A.T. words actually pop-out at the right time instead of during Scrabble games or in crossword puzzles. Mrs. Milliard would be proud.) Propinquity means "individuals affiliate with one another because of spatial or geographical proximity, forming groups based on nearness." Obviously, high-school loyalty creates group association because of the proximity, but it's only a loose formation, because leadership is necessary to find a common cause or purpose—the *why*. What high-school student does not have propinquity and loyalty to the mascot, simply because he or she attends the school? The sense of a belonging to something larger than yourself is like building a sense of community—a sense of belonging to something.

On top of new leadership and building the four C's—communication, connection, commitment, and caring—the coaching staff has its hands tied by the state high-school rule of "no direct baseball instruction in the off-season, conditioning excepted." You would have a full-scale company revolt from not only the workforce but also the stockholders with yearly leadership departures, and yet every year, like returning Capistrano swallows, an entire new leadership and yearling group arrives. How do you maintain a culture this way, getting the right people on the bus and in the right seats?

The round-about ways to help sustain culture, develop new leaders, and maintain team cohesion are leadership classes, discussion groups, and reading lists. Coach Kevin Eastman puts it succinctly: "Getting there requires you first get in. Get in the fight. Get in the hours. Get in the work. Get in the study. Get in the mindset." Another analogy for the leadership transfer is track and field relay racers who hand a baton to their next teammate as the relay team moves on. Slogans, logos, symbols, and common language all serve as lore to hand to the next team. One of our team's cultural hand-me-down symbols is an old auto tire. "We're like a used tire. You can try to wear us out, throw us out, drive over us, hit us, trash us, rip us, and tear us, but like a discarded used tire, we're still here and fighting." Call the tire part of our re-cycle program.

What are the results? Since the staff started implementing the development phases, we see a remarkable change in team development, especially through the shared conditioning sessions, which allow emerging leaders to set examples, encourage others, and develop team order or roles. I do not have statistics, business intelligence measures, sample variances, or binomial coefficients on our results. There are no Sabermetrics measuring team culture of which I am aware. What we do have is anecdotal testaments and general observations. We use the season to *prove*, and the off-season and practice to *improve*.

President John F. Kennedy once said, "Leadership and learning are indispensable to each other." Leadership development should be an on-going learning process. I firmly believe leadership can be taught, whether in the crucible of experience, through mentoring, or through the classroom.

This last year provides unequivocal evidence that our process is working and improving. Returning from a particularly hard-fought loss to an archrival, a game we should have won, the bus ride was somber, more like the prayerful quiet you'd find at a memorial service. The head coach noticed one player taking the loss particularly hard; he was somewhat red-eyed. Knowing this is not the typical eighteen-year-old, "I'm my own man and a seasoned veteran" reaction, the coach took to consoling the player. Sure, the player stated that he was sad about the game, but in the prior minutes, he had received a text message that his pet dog was lost and that his family had been searching for it over for the past two to three hours. Upon hearing their teammate's distress, instead of going home immediately for a shower, dinner, homework, and/or relaxation, a group of ten or so players went to this teammate's neighborhood to search for the dog. After a short search, and because of the sheer number of searchers, they found the dog. The lesson of "we before me" manifested in a simple, small act of charity on an otherwise ordinary day.

The opportunities to make a difference, to give back, are so obvious that sometimes they are hard to see. Your self-perception is rarely accurate. This is why seeking feedback is so important. "Feedback is the breakfast of champions." Sincere feedback from a peer needs to be looked at as a short-cut to success, and in a transformational team, readily accepted.

Otherwise you can lock yourself into the repetitive "could've, would've, should've" cycle. My decision to jump into coaching seemed a logical extension, and it was my turn to "step up" and try to make a difference, even if the learning curve was near vertical.

Words cannot adequately express the joys and lows in the seasonal roller-coaster ride. What a ride! What an addiction! The only comparable event I can relate it to happened during my Air Force air-refueling days. My crew and I were refueling four fighter aircraft halfway over the Atlantic. Behind on fuel and having to receive fuel from another tanker or face a remote island diversion, everyone—my tanker and the four fighters—needed me to complete our refueling. The mission's success depended on my performing a difficult skill, with no alternative and no one else to perform it. Maneuvering to contact a refueling boom from another aircraft in smooth, daylight conditions is hard enough, but in marginal visibility and turbulence, when crossing the Atlantic with no one else able to take over, it is a definite "you have to perform or we fail" situation. This ain't no roller coaster, and it ain't no ride. This was real, and we could not pull over to the side of the road and think about alternatives. Yoda's quote, "Do or do not; there is no try" was never more applicable. Coaching a team to success, I get the same adrenaline rush and sense of satisfaction. Baseball teaches so many life lessons. And who wouldn't want to ride the coaster?

Someone suggested that I try my hand at substitute teaching. Incredulously, I said, "Can I do that?" The enthusiastic answer was, "Heck yeah! (At least, I think it was heck yeah. It could have been a similar word. I am not sure. I was excited about the prospect.) You just need to apply with your resume and attend an orientation day at the school-district administration building."

Anyway, substitute teaching is a mixed bag, ranging from exciting history topics, British literature, and poetry to class caretaker, but oh … what a difference in quality between the Seattle "at-risk" students and the local high school's students, especially in demeanor and discipline. Most days, I enjoyed the classes, but interaction with the teachers and staff was at a formal, polite distance, so I did not last long. I am a big extrovert, and the occasional aloofness definitely places me as an outsider.

With my limited interaction with the teachers, I felt an undercurrent of palpable fear of the administration, even though what I saw was only the lower right-hand corner of the big picture. The teachers seemed competent, with an underlying desire for continuous improvement, but the "silo" mentality was evident and initiatives were stifled. Why not embrace the teachers as valuable assets instead of mere cogs in the education machinery? An African proverb says, "If you want to go fast, go alone. If you want to go far, go together." It's a wise proverb.

The point being that there is a definitive difference between working for a boss and working for a leader. Positive leadership lets you go far, because they inspire rather than force with threats. I credit Alan Stein Jr. for putting team synergy in simple terms:

1 + 1 = 2 —> boss-employee relationship
1 + 1 = 3 —> servant leadership

Teams can be successful in a boss-employee relation, but when leaders inspire, you perform at a level no one thought possible.

When not substitute teaching, I took to tutoring students during the equivalent of an enhanced study hall twice a week. At first, I wasn't sure what to make of tutoring math, chemistry, and biology, and had doubts about my ability to relate back to Pythagoras, Avogadro, and Darwin. My strength was always history, literature, and (kind of) math and engineering. Over the last few years, I have definitely related to Edgar Alan Poe's "The Raven's" opening line: "Once upon a midnight dreary..."

The fear was that the students might find out that what I still knew from high school might fill a thimble. I knew the knowledge would come back, and maybe I could even have an opportunity to prepare. *Take a deep breath. Breathe out the past and inhale the future. Visualize success. Be positive.* I wanted to embrace the challenge (not to be confused with "fake it till you make it"). I knew I would be alright; I just needed to get the "first game" jitters out, and this reaction was a normal one.

What I actually found out was that the tutoring was pretty tame and mundane, bordering on ennui. The students would split up into groups and tutor themselves. All I needed to do was monitor and guide the groups for eight hours a day, with a lunch break that was not long enough to go anywhere. The tutoring did not last long, only about four months.

The students readily accepted me, and I even had a few compliments, such as "You explain blah, blah, blah really well." However, the eight hours of observing students tutoring themselves just did not work for an extrovert who likes conversations. Meanwhile, the substitute teaching was better, especially if the teacher made the next day's lesson available so I could prepare some. I would have stayed with subbing if more teachers made their lessons available prior to the sub day.

My goal remained in this venue. I wanted to make a difference by mentoring, not replacing, the teacher who had better skills and knowledge than I did. My frustration stemmed from knowing I had something to contribute, *if* I could prepare. My pilot training days taught me the six P's: "Piss poor planning promotes poor performance." However, with generally no pre-lesson direction, the subbing became more of a babysitting job. "Play this video and handout this worksheet." The other downside was the lack of acknowledgment, much less engagement, from the full-time teachers. But then building relationship is such a key to a strong organization, and I was an outsider.

I felt I needed to accept what I was—baseball coach, tutor, and occasional substitute teacher—or go back to being a kept man, gigolo, or trophy husband. Nah. I was "too old" for those roles.

My off-season search for something fulfilling led me to the nearby Civil Air Patrol (CAP). With my twenty-year service in the Air Force and Air Force Reserve, maybe I could contribute in some measure to any or all of the CAP functions of emergency services, aerospace education, and cadet programs for those twelve- to eighteen-year-olds. Certainly, a teaching role might present itself in STEM, aviation, character development, or Air Force history. So, I joined and continue to mentor the cadets and occasionally the senior members on various subjects.

In addition to aerospace education, I began learning about the emergency services possibilities with CAP. Emergency services for CAP involves a lot of aviation and ground-incident-response-related activities. One course in particular opened my eyes, which directly related to Federal Emergency Management incidents and disaster-response teams, called the Incident Command System. The CAP process looked onerous, but I noticed the Illinois Fire Institute offered a five-day course in downtown Chicago. The course was challenging, trying to cram five pounds of information into a one-pound bag, but I managed to complete it. I learned so much about the National Incident Command System and how the laws, rules, and regulations governed who was in-charge of incidents, ranging from hurricane recovery and natural disasters to train chemical spills and forest fires. Happily, the plan works in concert with all the agencies involved.

I have strived all along to find a place to remain relevant and avoid "Geezerville." I needed (and continue to need) a place to make a difference. It is kind of like being at a bus station and looking for a destination. You just need to find the right bus and a driver.

11 – MY ONE WORD: MENTOR

"A mentor is someone who allows you
to see the hope inside yourself."
—Oprah Winfrey

Boredom, frustration, and feeling ineffectual ... these are factors to overcome when thinking about the future. All these are based on fear of the future. Like Jon Gordon likes to point out, "Fear or faith both deal with a future that has not happened. If it has not happened, why would you pick fear? Why not have faith? Fear causes you to focus on your problems. Faith helps you find and seek solutions."

Experiencing fear is okay; everyone experiences fear. Fear is a natural reaction, but if it takes over, it can lead to inaction, depression, or worse. Even the bravest of heroes feel fear. How you control or overcome fear greatly influences the outcome. Why, through inaction, would you choose not to influence the outcome?

Sometimes, overcoming fear just takes time, and maybe (after a traumatic event) you really do have to go through the seven stages of grief. My experience seemed to cover all those stages, with some looping back and repeating. I went through shock and denial a couple of times, like when I learned I would never fly again. Pain and guilt are normal, and I definitely could not rely on alcohol to counter the pain with my condition. The anger and bargaining manifested in "Why me?" for a while. Isolation and downright loneliness reoccurred. From my previous writing, you can see signs of the upward turn and reconstruction, or at least attempts to return to a semblance of the job where I never felt like I worked a day. Did I ever reach acceptance? Yes. I think I have with coaching, speaking, and making a difference. I have written more with this book than I ever have. (My editor says to keep it coming, because it's good for business, but stop using double negatives. "Don't never use double negatives" was great advice.)

Depression, though, is a funny thing. You can have it but not know it. You can know it but not have it. The sadness can be the most oppressive feeling, like the proverbial "dark cloud" that won't go away. Depression can be hard to detect in yourself, and sometimes in others. I've struggled with it at various times, and I've found that serving others is a great way to climb out of it. The questions remain: "How do you know you're making progress? Why are we afraid to ask for help? Why do people avoid you when you have depression, especially since having it is the exact time you need someone?" Most people would rather twist screwdrivers into their eyes while chugging a gallon of gasoline than go through depression. To take care of depression, I am like Yogi Berra, "I take a two-hour nap every day from twelve until three."

The best way I've found to deal with it (DWI, there it is again) is through service to others. An attitude of gratitude is what sustains me. I figure that, if I'm still here, I must have a purpose to make a difference. Muhammed Ali once said, "Service to others is the rent you pay for your room on Earth." I figure that, for me, every day past October 14, 2008 is a gift, and I need to make sure rent is paid on time. I mean, don't tick off the landlord (God). Right?

Recently, I came upon an opportunity to make a difference year-round, a way to convey a compelling story in such a way as to make a difference. Through yet another edification process, I became certified as Jon Gordon Power of Positive Leadership trainer, now able to teach/facilitate workshops. Straight from the covered curriculum, my goal is facilitating, helping individuals, teams, and organizations focus on nurturing the roots of their organizational tree while maintaining the fruit production.

Positive leadership inspires employees to accomplish more than they ever thought possible. Grant Cardone alludes to positive leadership in his book, *The 10X Rule,* as a fundamental element to dreaming and obtaining ten times (10X) what you originally thought possible. This training fits neatly into my "one word"—the word on which I base my focus and decisions. My one word is "mentor," and it motivates me to spread the positive. Does it mean I will change everyone's leadership style? No. But just like one word, maybe I change one person at a time, one day at a time.

In my most inspirational and positive moments, I realize that today is a gift, and I have a newfound desire to make a difference for someone, to help someone find his telescope view. I want to help them figure out and identify their North Star, their *why*, breaking their journey to it into daily, microscopic steps and tasks. So how do you find your purpose—your *why*? How do you stay motivated? Some people have credos, mission statements, and some have nothing.

Finding your motive is the single-most important motivator toward a long- or short-range goal. A good metaphor for purpose is that you start out as an acorn, small but with lots of potential. Short term, the acorn's goals are to drop to the ground, get covered with dirt, absorb the rain, find sunlight, develop a taproot, and gradually sprout a shoot that becomes a sapling and grows into a massive oak tree. The acorn's long-term purpose is growing into a sturdy oak tree. What is interesting is that acorns fail to germinate when close to the parent tree, because not enough sunlight penetrates the parent's canopy, so it must be transported by squirrels and animals to another area in order to thrive.

How do you define your goals or purpose? Some people may start each year with a New Year's resolution, but most resolutions are too cumbersome and difficult to remember, as long sentences, paragraphs, or lists. A New Year's resolution can give you a sense of purpose or direction for the year, if you can keep it in front of you. An interesting fact, though: Over 50 percent of New Year's resolutions are forgotten and waylaid by the end of January, most probably because the resolution is difficult to remember in its entirety.

A simpler method is boiling down your purpose into one word. The book *One Word Which Will Change Your Life*, by Dan Britton, Jimmy Page, and Jon Gordon, breaks down a method for creating your one word. The method uses personal introspection, meditation, prayer, and other activities in an effort to get you in that cognitive zone where your best "aha" moments occur. The *One Word Which Will Change Your Life* method led me to my one word, "mentor," for this year.

Mentor's verb definition is "to advise or train someone, especially a younger colleague," and it certainly simplifies things. The word "mentor" comes from the Greek name *Mentor*, who was the adviser to a young Telemachus in Homer's *Odyssey*, and I believe "advisor" fits perfectly. Rather than a long credo or tagline, which is hard to keep in your forefront or even memorize, a single word describing your guide for the year is simple. One word is easily captured on sticky notes, can be placed as a reminder on your mirror, or located in any number of highly visible places. I keep mine on my work desk. I embrace the idea, as it gives me a *why*, a purpose, and a goal for the coming year.

To find your one word is not a difficult process. Growth-mindset people use personal thinking time to hash out ideas, solve problems, and make plans. All you need is to find a quiet place to contemplate without distractions. Almost like meditating, sooner or later, as your mind drifts into the wonderful, inspirational mental zone, you can capture what your theme will be and massage it into one word. I was skeptical the first time I tried this, but I did have my "aha" moment, and "mentor" popped into to my head.

"Mentor" fits nicely into coaching, facilitating, keynote speaking, instructing cadets, and facilitating workshops. How better to fulfill the purpose of making a difference? Building and maintaining relationships is the key to leadership and followership, and if I can pass that on while teaching and facilitating, am I not making a difference?

The hardest part of mentoring is guiding (rather than imparting to) those you mentor. According to psychologist Carol Dweck, the best mentors engage their business/academic/sports teams' growth mindsets with the continuous improvement of possibilities over a fixed mindset. No easy task for the mentor, but then I am only beginning to embrace the mentor's growth mindset. If my goal as a mentor is making a difference, then I need a growth mindset. Yes, another goal, but it will require improving my leadership one step at a time. When you drive at night, your headlights only shine on the next two hundred feet and, really, in the day time when you drive you can only take care of the next two hundred feet. I'm taking care of the next two hundred feet. Correct?

A growth mindset needs to be developed, instilled, and periodically sharpened. The mindset can dull or disappear completely without regular maintenance. Leaders become complacent without regular sharpening. Since leadership skills cannot be measured objectively, and create no data, the progress of these skills doesn't really show and are hard to quantify. Recurrent workshop and current leadership publications can help but require an open mind to absorb better ways.

Leaders with fixed mindsets may be slow to accept new leadership skills and new capabilities for reasons such as self-protection or ego. "I know that" or "I've seen that before" are justifications for lack of change. Many of the leadership skills seem so obvious that fixed-mindset participants assume they already know a skill or believe their leadership skills are a given fact. Rather than searching for the best leadership, the fixed-mindset coaches think the skills they have are "good enough."

"Good enough" is not good enough. Satisfaction with the current state is not part of mentoring. Guidance, motivation, emotional support, and role modeling are instrumental to coaching. A good mentor makes a difference.

12 – DEAL WITH IT

"You're not here to survive this;
you're here to take charge of it."
—U.S. Navy SEALs

God has a plan. I just wish sometimes He would let me peek at it, or maybe He has let me peek, and I am not smart enough to see it. You know the feeling you get when you're coming to a fork in the road? You can take one path or the other, and yet, you often find yourself back at the same place. A Buddhist saying goes like this: "You can't control the future. The past is already done, so live the moment...." It boils down to a fancy way of rephrasing the Navy SEAL saying: "Deal with it (DWI)."

There was a brief time after my Wisconsin job where I was not dealing with it very well, if at all. The aftereffects of being gone for long stretches of time continued to linger. I struggled with my new role, as Heidi started prospecting for other nursing opportunities, and it led to some heavy-duty conflict. It got so bad that we started going to a counselor, and it was amazing what we found out about each other. We really needed (mostly I needed) to understand how hard the other was trying to be a good spouse. Somehow, we were blinded by our preconceived notions.

Not to get too personal, but neither of us realized how concerned we were about growing older. An ironic exchange during one session had Heidi telling the counselor that my problem was that I wanted to be back flying and traveling so much so that I could be back with all the twenty-five-year-old flight attendants. The counselor turned to me and said, "Do you think that?" and I replied directly to Heidi, "No, I don't want a twenty-five-year-old; all I want is you." I think the discussion driving home was definitely better than any counseling session. We laughed pretty hard and maybe shed a few tears. It did not completely resolve our issues yet, but it did change our perspective. We eventually worked out most of our issues. Married people know you always have issues to work on.

I still had to deal with all the time on my hands, because baseball coaching only occupied part of the year. Baseball season lasts from March until mid–July. So, from mid–July to end of February becomes a tough period. I'm going on twelve years since my life-changing epiphany, and I am well past the cardiac doctor's long-term prognosis of ten-year survivability. So, how do I deal with it? I decided a while back that I needed to embrace my roles: baseball coach, mentor, speaker, and house husband. Too much time on my hands leads to thinking about my mortality. In my darkest moments, I don't feel like I have much time left, or believe I won't get to say goodbye to someone close, or think maybe I'll fail to meet an obligation. I am so lucky to even be here, and if not for the commitment of the EMTs, nurses, and doctors … well, it's a miracle.

My latest challenge involved building referrals and booking speaking engagements. The Power of Positive Leadership training provides the presentation material but no marketing. I had dealt with large and small presentations before, to wildly diverse groups of Kenyans, Filipinos pilots, Cape Verdean aviation managers, and others, but never marketing. The questions loom regarding where to find the referrals or why businesses, athletic teams, or organizations might want to hear me speak on any subject, much less on leadership in a workshop.

I dove in with social media postings on Facebook, Twitter, and Instagram. Advertising, promotions, ads, and boosts became the norm. With no ready help, I immersed myself in the subtleties of clicks, likes, impressions, and the like. I sent out hundreds of personalized letters and emails to business leaders, educators, athletic directors, and numerous people through the chamber of commerce, with follow-ups. I sent especially personalized emails to previous directors and VPs. I created several one- to two-minute videos using little snippets of allegorical material, describing what my workshops and keynote talks are about. The importance of a bold, compelling, and personal story is of utmost importance when trying to captivate a following.

Mentally comparing myself to the all-weather, 200,000-mile radial tire, neither over-inflated nor under-inflated, I strive to stay positive and stay the course, making this my mantra as the steady stream of rejections and non-responsiveness continues unabated. I don't look at how tough the situation is but rather remain tough facing the situation, because whining and complaining don't help you deal with it or stay positive. Dealing with it requires adjusting, adapting, and most of all, improvising.

According to Yamamoto Tsunetomo, in his book *Hagakure: The Book of the Samurai*, "There is succession of moment after moment. There will be nothing else to do and nothing else to pursue. Live being true to the single purpose of the moment." It's another fancy way of saying "take care of the next two hundred feet," but keep the goal, your *why*, and your purpose in mind.

Still, the next two hundred feet have their obstacles—sorry, *opportunities*. Opportunities can be like traffic lights. If we are approaching a traffic light, and it is green, we continue normally, at the same speed, almost unthinking. But if the light turns yellow, we can react one of two ways: Either we slow down and stop, or we speed up to make it through the intersection. Speeding up has a downside, which is that we run the risk of a collision with crossing traffic or a ticket for running through a red light. Obviously, we stop for a red light. Recognizing our traffic lights in decision-making is very important as we take care of the next two hundred feet. We can proceed toward our goals as long as we recognize our traffic lights and have a planned, consistent reaction when we see a yellow light.

The goal is hard to keep in front of the everyday clutter. Taking care of the everyday clutter, the distractions, and the "pop-ups" can detract from your long-term goals, or your daily goals, and may require course corrections. Remember the "hundreds of ways to drive to Disney World" analogy? Lewis Carroll's *Alice in Wonderland* puts it this way: "One day Alice came to a fork in the road and saw a Cheshire cat in a tree. 'Which road do I take?' she asked. 'Where do you want to go?' was his response. 'I don't know,' Alice answered. 'Then,' said the cat, 'it doesn't matter.'" My problem all along was deciding which road I wanted to take.

But it *does* matter. The frustrations mount but success comes to those who work and remain undeterred. Jon Gordon, talking about your *why*, or purpose, says, "We don't burn out with what we do. We burn out because we forget why we do it." So, I deal with "what's important next" while "living true to the moment." I need to do this on my own. The Irish adage, "You've got to do your own growing, no matter how tall your grandfather was" comes to mind. My plan, the plan, gets altered as course corrections necessitate, but the goal remains to "mentor," to make a difference, to help others.

Since my intention is to make a difference, it was no surprise when the name of my business came to me: "Be A Bean." My spiel would be, "Like a coffee bean, which smells good, tastes good, and positively changes the water around it, let me show you how to be a coffee bean and transform your team from ordinary water into gourmet coffee. How about a leadership workshop to better your communications to build trust, gain commitment, and increase caring, making a difference on your productivity and bottom line? Be a bean; be a transformer." I figured public speaking about my experiences should start making a difference, but it takes a lot of work and a lot of rejection.

Success never comes all at once, and honestly, you never truly arrive at success. I do not think success is ever obtained, but rather that success is found within the process. Think of those whom you consider successful. They are successful because they continue to work at success. Michelangelo created numerous masterpieces; Thomas Edison developed many key inventions; Michael Jordan earned six NBA Championship rings; and Maya Angelou wrote more than one famous poem. Resting on your laurels does not make you successful, but continuous improvement and trusting the process makes for success. The definition for my success is making a difference by getting to a performance level I never thought possible, through daily goals and long-term goals. Daily goals are an important personal metric on your progress toward your telescope goal. Spending the day without two to three daily goals equates to spending time on a stationary exercise bike. You can go ten to fifteen miles on a stationary bike, and you're still in the same place. No matter what your job is, you can get consumed with the constant "pop-ups" and daily busy work, all the while remaining in place. But if I want a sense of accomplishment, a sense of progress toward my goal, I need some daily objectives.

Rather than riding a stationary bike every day, keep your ultimate goal, your telescopic view, in mind. Deal with today and make your metric a recounting of a daily goals.

"Finish each day and be done with it. You have done what
you could. Some blunders and absurdities no doubt crept
in; forget them as soon as you can. Tomorrow is a new day.
You shall begin it serenely and without too high a spirit to be
encumbered with your old nonsense."
—Ralph Waldo Emerson

The only take away from your blunders is the lesson
moving forward.

In the truest sense, I need Navy SEAL improvising.
Acquiring new snappy business cards is a start, followed by a
podium banner. My idea is to create podcast shows, promoting my speaking. Like the eighteenth-century English Navy
press gangs recruiting sailors, I kidnap my cinematography and
sound-design sons to aid in creating these new videos. In actu-
ality, my sons readily want to help (for little or no fee, but scale
is scale and they are professionals). These guys turn my mish-
mash of video ideas and scripts into a finished, professional-
looking presentation. I get cut out of most podcasts they film.
My sons say it improves the cinematography.

My foray into professional speaking continues with mixed
results, and every day, I incorporate what I've learned. I jumped
feet first into social-media advertising, website design, finding
public speaking facilities/accommodations, and payment apps.
I interviewed several advertising-management companies, but
the costs at this stage were prohibitive. Besides, I seem to learn
most of my lessons the hard way.

On one occasion, I gave my signature speech to a group
I had joined using my interpretation of the group's standard
template. It was a template that encourages you to use an
opening story that inspires, talk about the usual three main
points, tell another story, and then provide the take-aways,
hooking the audience to your business, all in a mere twenty

minutes. Well, my speech was a miss, according to the critique. The speaking group is a great place for trying out your shtick, because in a loving manner, the group holds you accountable to a high standard. The group liked my animated delivery and some of the stories, but I overwhelmed them with too much jargon and too many acronyms. Back to the drawing board I go to make the adjustments.

The biggest lesson over the course of the last year perfectly illustrates "the difference" between success and lesson learned. I designed and published my website using one of many self-help web-design companies. This company has numerous templates and macro-programs to aide in creating a page. I tried several different templates in an attempt to optimize my brand. Each template had a save function so you could compare the results before choosing your final design and input. I narrowed mine down to two choices and eventually published one of them. My final choice contained a splash page, banner, thumbnails, business description, bio, and testimonials. I received numerous compliments on the professional look.

I used the web address on my correspondence and business card. All my emails contained the URL for the site ... or so I thought. The usual hyperlink format looks something like www.xyz.net, which is what I had in my email signature block. Unfortunately, that format drove clients to a saved web design and not the actual published page. What I found out was the format needed an additional forward slash as in www.xyz.net/ to get to the actual published page. I will get into that in more depth further in the book, but a forward slash (/) was "that difference." This was another learning experience: the possibly comical omission of the slash, since the link led to one of my proposed incomplete web-page edits. Ah, what are you going to do? Fix it and go on to "what's important next."

13 – CHALLENGE OR OPPORTUNITY

"If a window of opportunity appears,
don't pull down the shade."
—Tom Peters

The steel-making process first involves smelting. "Smelting involves heating up raw ore until the metal becomes spongy, and the chemical compounds in the ore begin to break down."[1] The elements in the iron ore are boiling out or burned off in the heating process. Steel only becomes tempered by going through the smelting process.

Much like the smelting process, successful people are tempered through the success-failure process. I always said my failures far outnumbered my successes, but I always savored my successes. I came to realize that failure is a part of improving and nothing improves without going through the process. "Fall down seven times, stand up eight."

In retrospect, I regularly entered the smelting crucible, but if you have a growth mindset, you look at obstacles and challenges as opportunities to learn and improve. Out of high school, I failed entry to the Air Force Academy, but I redoubled my effort, went to a preparatory school, and was accepted the

---

1   Marshall Brain and Robert Lamb, "How Iron and Steel Work." 1 April 2000. HowStuffWorks.com. Accessed 1 June 2020, https://science. howstuffworks.com/iron.htm.

following year. My aviation career included several less-than-stellar check rides, but I got the opportunity to correct and learn from them. Events outside of my control occurred that presented extreme financial and personal risks, such as airline mergers, the first and second Gulf Wars, threats of labor strikes, an airline crash with personal friends onboard, 9/11, the recession of 2007, my heart attack in 2008, being let go from a job, and on and on.

I always forget that the origins of many of my habits, routines, and rituals were instilled in me from my Air Force Academy days over forty-five years ago. Making my bed every day, leaving the room cleaner than I found it, drawers with "inspection-worthy" folded underwear in neat rows…. All of the lessons and habits I learned back then are so deeply rooted that I carry this sense of personal tidiness to this day. Admiral William H. McRaven wrote a book and gave a commencement speech to the University of Texas's 2014 graduating class on this very subject, titled "Make Your Bed." The gist of the benefit of the routine is the immediate sense of accomplishment in doing something, in completing something as your very first step of the day and completing it well.

Some of these routines and habits are often looked down upon and labeled anal retentive, meticulous, and overly detailed-oriented. I disagree. People who develop positive routines can automatically respond to situations without having to figure out a new process, and therefore, can think about more pressing issues. Experience is another way of building routines. How many lessons do we have where the moral of our story becomes, "Well, I'll never do that again?" or "I got things out of order, and I should have stuck with my routine."

One of the graduation requirements for military S.E.R.E. is completing survival, evasion, resistance, and escape (S.E.R.E.) training. It's not even close to all that SEAL or other extremely difficult military-training programs include, but it is a part of SEAL training and a requirement for military pilots. I learned valuable lessons from S.E.R.E.

I could tell you all the stereotypical S.E.R.E. training survival stories. For example, the one about losing twenty-five pounds in two weeks. I could afford to do now, but back then, I was a twenty-year-old, lean, mean legitimate tough guy (L.T.G.) with almost no fat reserves. I can tell stories about cooking with my Michelin-rated sous chef, preparing chipmunk with a water and wild onion sauce—although we didn't have wine to pair with it, we did get to try snake blood. Yummy! I believe Gordon Ramsey would've kicked us out of the kitchen. I even got to do mountain orienteering using a compass and map during the evasion phase of S.E.R.E. It would have been challenging and fun but for being chased by bad guys whose goal was to throw you back into the POW camp if caught.

What I want to concentrate on is the POW and evasion/border crossing lessons.

Lesson 1 is how to handle stressful waiting with no controllables. The POW phase started in a darkened theater where we sat for some six to eight hours. Talking and bathroom visits were not allowed. If you were caught talking, the guards removed you from the theater, and you were never seen again (at least for this phase of training). We all knew at some point we would end the day in the POW camp, but watching talkers disappear kept most of us from talking. I am sure I was like the rest of my group thinking, *Keep your mouth closed and maybe you can reduce the time in the POW camp.* Like the rest, though, alone with our thoughts, there was the ever-present dread of what the next phase would be like. Would we be beaten? Would we hold up or cave under pressure? Why was it taking so long? These were the questions racing through our minds.

Lesson 2 occurred after the survival and evasion/orienteering phase of daily checkpoints, navigating through the mountains with the threat of capture and return to the POW camp. On the last night, we had a border crossing from "bad guy" land to "neutral/good guy" land. As my group of three approached the dirt mountain road that night, we hid in some thick, thorny tumbleweed to observe and time the truck and foot patrols. Occasionally, in the distance, an unlucky evader would trip a flare, which would light up the night like the mid-day sun, but we continued to observe.

At one point, a truck patrol dismounted three border guards with rifles and flashlights. The guards randomly scanned the bush with their flashlights, occasionally shouting various epithets. One of the guards shone a light in my direction and then started running in my direction, shouting, "I see one!" Without thinking, my reaction was immediate, and I started running in the dark in the opposite direction. Within twenty-five yards, I collided with a tree limb across my chest, knocking me to the ground with a resounding thud. Gasping for air, the thought of making too much noise and being captured only worsened my seemingly

loud attempts to breathe. The dread of returning to the POW camp was my foremost fear. I
did recover, evade capture, and finally crossed
the "border" uneventfully about two hours
later. Everyone has fears, anxiety, and negative
thoughts. How you corral those thoughts and
stay positive influences the outcome.

With apologies to Paul McLean for altering his scientific
names, I will take some liberties now with outlining how our
minds work. Basically, we have three mindsets:

1. **Reptilian Mind** - the automatic functions of breathing,
   heartbeat, hungry, cold—the self-centered part.
2. **Monkey Mind** - records memories, behaviors—both
   agreeable and disagreeable ones—and is responsible for
   emotions. It's the kid-like reactions, if you will—the fly,
   fight, or freeze.
3. **Jedi Mind** - human language, abstract thought, intuition, and consciousness. It is the mind that develops
   reasoning the best by what is called exposure therapy,
   through lessons learned.

How we approach events, problems, and relations depends
on which mind is in use. The discipline we've developed and
lessons we've learned are key components. If time is a factor in
developing a response, then a Jedi uses plans and checklists to
shorten reaction time. For instance, pilots have quick-response
checklists to address most time-critical events. If you have
the foresight to see a possible event, then you have a plan for
the contingency.

Dr. R. L. Helmreich's Threat and Error Management model
applies to how we use our three minds. We cannot control
when, where, what, or how events come before us, but when

the event threatens us, the best strategies through our Jedi mind are to avoid, trap, or mitigate the threat before it turns into a negative outcome. We can avoid the bad outcomes through plans, protocols, or rules to reduce the possibility of a negative outcome. If we cannot avoid the threat, we can trap it by returning the situation to (at least) a stable condition, and then work on improving the situation or at least mitigate the negative outcome. Controlling the controllables by timely recognition of approaching events, events that are happening, and events that could happen is another way of defining avoid, trap, and mitigate.

Time available (from immediate action to time to ponder) is the first consideration. With a little time, experience is a great teacher and pre-set plans are essential. You need to stabilize the situation, identify the problem, and take appropriate action. With more time, you can add a layer in which you gather information, develop a plan, execute, re-evaluate the results, and if necessary, alter the plan until you recover.

From my S.E.R.E. experience, I carried forward two pertinent threat and error lessons, and no, you do not have to go to S.E.R.E. training to learn them:

1. The need to control my anxiety—dread if you will—while waiting in the theater auditorium, a basic fear of the future with little control except my response to the future and controlling my reptile mind.
2. Overriding my monkey mind during the border crossing, overriding my fly, fight, or freeze syndrome using my Jedi mind.

Both the dread while waiting and border-crossing experiences were learning experiences I can refer to when similar events occur.

The Navy SEAL adage is "Tonight, you will have to be your very best. You must rise above your fears, your doubts, and your fatigue. No matter how dark it gets, you must complete the mission. This is what separates you from everyone else."

What does that imply? No one escapes events. Events are completely out of our control. What our response is can influence the outcome. Even no response influences the outcome, because you absolve yourself of influencing the outcome. In other words, whatever happens, happens. A positive response, a "what's important next" (W.I.N.) or "deal with it" (D.W.I.) mentality, is the best approach; it means you are working on a solution. Jon Gordon summarizes the importance of our response through an equation:

Event + Positive Response = Outcome (E+P=O)

As I am writing this, the world is dealing with the COVID-19 virus—anecdotally, an event allegedly started by someone eating undercooked bat of all things. Who knew such a small act would have the profound consequence of the worldwide pandemic we face today? Social distancing, voluntary quarantines, and mandatory quarantines are now familiar terms to all.

The toll the virus has taken as it ravages country after country is incredible. It has caused cancellations of school-year activities, classroom learning, and sports programs. When we told our baseball players the season was suspended indefinitely, it was hard to watch seventeen- and eighteen-year-old men, who had worked their tails off in the preceding ten months, visibly weep. We did remind them of the suffering and deaths due to the virus, and we tried to console them. We spoke of the legacy of leadership and hard work they were leaving behind them, a legacy they would leave for the underclass team members in years to come. The lesson was hard, but we did overhear familiar language, expressions of "let's deal with it" and "let's move on to what's important next," as they chose to protect our families and players.

In the community, we are witness to the gamut of reactions from "whatever happens, happens" to inspiring individuals adjusting to the new norm. One example is a hairstylist offering virtual haircuts for a price as he guides you via a video-conference. Another is my brother-in-law, who is conducting violin lessons to a group from Sweden via the Internet for a fee. Plus, who cannot credit the incredible healthcare providers' responses? These are great examples of dealing with adversity and making the best of the circumstances, turning challenges into new opportunities.

14 – WHY I COACH

"Leadership is a matter of having people look at you
and gain confidence seeing how you react.
If you're in control, they're in control."
—Tom Landry

What I found rewarding over my limited years of coaching is the players who come back and show gratitude, knowing the lessons learned were lifetime lessons. Billy Graham said it best: "A coach will affect more players in a year than an ordinary person will in a lifetime." You may not reach all of them, but if you reach one at a time on a daily basis, you make a difference. The current players I coach get it. They realize that, in this season (or any season), there is only one overall champion, and if you are not the championship team, it does not mean the team has failed. The truest measures remain: Did this team perform above what they thought they were capable of performing? Did the team have fun? Did the team members discover something about their character and improve? For me as a coach, did I affect all the players in a positive way?

Making a difference with those I coach is a central tenet to my coaching style. I wish I could say I am innovative or communicate a new way to approach player development. The best I can say is that I learned (and adapted) from some of the best. Since experience is the best teacher, and it supposedly takes ten years to be considered a master at a job, I have a ways to go. Here's the thing though: I never want to stop getting better.

Most coaches start out imitating coaches who impressed them in the past, and the old style of "benevolent dictator" seems like the most common approach. Books, webinars, and conferences can add skills, but there is simply no substitute for actual experience. I wish we had simulators for coaches to experience coaching in real conditions. The next best thing is your current head coach or leader allowing real-time game decision experience and/or having a dedicated mentor who wants to make a difference and not just win games. Yet there is so much more that coaches do off the field and away from the games. Disciplining for infractions, managing disgruntled parents, fundraising, and tackling field improvements all take time to handle. The actual coaching on the field is just the most fun and challenging duty.

On the other hand, the most rewarding part of coaching is the effect you have on the players. For example, most players are used to the traditional post-game critique/rehash:

"Why did you miss the cutoff guy? Did you notice the trailing runner advanced to second and ended up scoring later in the inning? You guys missed two bunt signs. We gotta do better."

After my first head junior varsity game where we had a tough lost 3–2, I started the post-game talk with:

"What did we do good in this game?"

Followed by a direct question to each player:

"What did you learn this game?"

After a round of answers, I talked about the next game, who would pitch, and ended with, "Okay, let's get ready for tomorrow."

We gathered together, gave one final cheer, and went home. The first game or two, I saw bewildered faces, but after those, I think they saw a distinct change in how we approach wins and losses. What's in the scorebook is done except for what we learned, and it was time to get on to the next important thing: the next game.

The mundane care for all the minute details can be mind-numbing for sure, in contrast to the exhilaration of coaching a game. You do need to be good at both facets of the job to be a good coach. I would imagine approaching the game duties is similar to the way, as kids, we approached going to school. If you go to any elementary school and watch the kids arrive and leave, they are excited—running and skipping. If you watch a high schooler, they walk with indifference and appear unenthusiastic while arriving and departing school. Why the change in eagerness? Might it be the repetitive drudge? A great coach will find a good way to maintain enthusiasm for the details and throughout the seasons.

Early on, I witnessed how a coach developed players who appeared not to be good players. One player comes to mind who was a yearly "cut" candidate or a marginal player who would warm the bench. Even in his last year of eligibility, he was a probable "cut." Coach "Murrdog" was the biggest proponent for keeping him on the team because of his work ethic, attitude, and team spirit. You could see him closing the holes in his game in his last year, with conditioning, an after-practice "just one more rep" mentality, and concentration on the getting the details.

You could refer to the guy almost cut as a "foxhole" guy, present next you, comfortable with his role, and working while he waited. This was a guy who was constantly growing and learning through the rejection and failures, and who, despite showing discomfort from his exposed vulnerability, continued to work and improve.

About a third of the way into his final season, he had an opportunity to start. He had two hits in three at bats and played so well that he became the starter for the rest of the season. This re-enforced the coach's resilience in looking at the intangibles of attitude, work ethic, role embracement, and team spirit. After four years of wanting to be part of something larger than himself, this player proved the point. He wanted to do what was best for the team instead what was best for him, and in the end, accomplished both.

Talent is only part of a player's make-up, with the other part being the character make-up. Teams carrying talented players who never embrace character development is like putting a cheap band-aid on a larger cut. Unless you can change the character, the cut will continue to bleed.

Lesson: The head coach was right about his potential, and I was wrong—a good lesson for the next marginal but potential player.

Do you want a talent versus culture example? Look at the Titanic story—not the movie but the gritty tale of the finest, most modern ship in the world, filled with a talented, hand-picked crew. The goal on the maiden voyage was to set a speed record crossing the Atlantic Ocean in six days. Despite seven warnings about dangerous icebergs in the Titanic's vicinity from several other ships, the crew ignored the warnings and surged ahead. One warning message was reportedly answered with the equivalent of "stop bothering us." Talent, equipment, and clear goals cannot, will not, and will never equate to good leadership and teamwork. The arrogance of the Titanic crew, builders, and owners preordained the ship's fate. It was not only the arrogance but also the lack of experience of working together—since this was the crew's first voyage together—that factored into the Titanic's fate.

Incumbent to player development and leadership development is what Dr. Cory Dobbs calls "mattering matters." Whether in business or athletics, a team only has so many starters or positions to fill. What you do with the non-starters and benchwarmers is important for the team's future performance, as well as its interim performance. Coaches and leaders can inspire team members by acknowledging the incremental improvements in individuals or various players.

My coaching philosophy leans toward creating an environment of guiding players in their own development. I want them to see their improvements, allowing them to make mistakes and then overcome them. I never know exactly when I have made an imprint on a player or made a difference. Every once in a while, I have my beached starfish moment, where I know I saved one player by returning him to the safety of the ocean. I remember one player encounter distinctly. The player was not one of our stars, and he was struggling with his hitting. We talked off and on about swing fundamentals, but one day I asked him, "You know those guys that have awful swings but still seem to do pretty well?" He nodded, so I continued. "How do they do that?"

He said, "I guess they just walk up and do it."

"So, just walk up and do it," I said. There was no parting of the clouds, no deep, echoing voice giving advice, but you could see a smile on his face and a slight swagger as he walked away. Now, he did not exactly change into the team star, but I think he enjoyed and respected himself more. I still enjoy that moment.

As a junior varsity (JV) staff coach, the mission, core values, and program culture are established. As a subordinate and developing team, we (the team and two coaches) need to ensure our goals dovetail with the program goals, but we still need our own identity and purpose. The question became, "How can we express our goal and our plan, with intentional growth built into the fabric?" Some teams suffer through season after season without clarity of purpose, like the Greek mythology story of

Sisyphus being sentenced to push the boulder up the hill only to have it roll back down the hill for eternity. "Nothing ever changes until you change, and everything changes once you change" is the perfect Facebook meme currently being *liked* and shared on social media.

During my first year as head JV coach, we had several guided discussions on what was important to the team—finding our *why*. One of the problems facing a JV team is that all the players desire to play at the varsity level, or feel they *belong* at the varsity level. Some of the players will move up to varsity, and some move down from varsity to JV. Next year's team development depends on experiencing the pressures and competition at the varsity level, and playing time for those varsity players who end up on the bench because someone is playing in front of them. So, we described our mission as developing our players to play at the varsity level as soon as possible, and to challenge teams we play to bring their "A" game, because they will see ours. It was simple and straight forward, allowing the players to see the purpose of the JV team in simple terms.

Aligning the players' goals of varsity playtime and bringing our "A" game every day is simple and achievable. A lot of teams make a state championship the goal. Here is the problem with a championship goal: Only one team will achieve the year's championship. If your team is not the champion, does it mean the year was unsuccessful? A team's goal must be achievable yet establish a reachable success. A state championship or a set number of wins is a result or a "fruit" and is a nice addition but cannot be the only measure of success.

Team survival and success relies on finding the right balance between focusing on the fruit, the bottom line, wins/losses, profit, revenue, and the foundational things, such as the health and strength of your culture. Imagine a different outcome if the Titanic captain, first mate, owner, or radio operator had been adamant about avoiding the dangerous icebergs. Imagine the outcome change if the culture was more open to feedback. To illustrate how subtle culture is, had someone ordered the Titanic to slow down, striking the iceberg may have never occurred. In that case, nothing measurable happened. Instead, all the "fruit" was present—a highly trained, talented crew with the latest equipment—but the culture was off, and it resulted in a tragic accident.

This year remains a mystery as to whether I made a difference. The tools I didn't use remain, gathering dust because of the unparalleled COVID-19 situation. After the shock of the 2020 season suspension, and possible complete cancellation, the goal remains, but the incomplete season, which never really started, is disconcerting. Did we, did I, make a difference this year? What can we do to get closure? Which of the little unused tools can I utilize?

The coaching staff set about arranging unique ways to stay connected during the period of social distancing, to maintain conditioning and skills to an extent but mostly to maintain or improve the team's bonds. We scheduled Zoom calls, sent text messages, and otherwise attempted to maintain connections. The effectiveness of webinars and school eLearning access remains to be seen. The motivation, so far, remains strong, and we have resolved to do just a little more than the next team. I spoke with the JV team on several occasions, attempting to leave them with something edifying about mental approaches or the importance of nutrition. I think the team absorbed some of the topics, even if the nutrition part was coming from an older, overweight coach.

(Side note: My will states that I am leaving my body to science, although I think there is a good chance that science will contest the will.)

We assume the bond between the current 2020 players remains strong. I don't know if I could stay motivated during this time if it were not for the example these men set. The 2020 team is leaving a legacy for the underclassmen. Talk about a "loaded team." It was full of "glue guys," the guys that bind a team. This team, as Coach "Murrdog" so aptly described them, may not have the finest talent around, but they are closer than any team he has coached, and "that's the difference."

They are a team in the sense that they can face adversity, because they have character and trust. Take a look at Google, as a company. They found out its best and most inventive team was not the most talented team but rather the team whose members felt emotionally safe. In other words, a team comprised of members who can trust each other, express themselves, and give and receive feedback for improvement rather than self-image protection, wants to become better. Quoted by many, it is a "we before me" philosophy. You cannot argue with Google's results. Interesting, if you search Bing for popular search terms, up comes Google. Wait. What?

Teams, like the Titanic crew, will face adversity at some point in the season. Coaches can sweep small transgressions away, but eventually, the small transgressions can build into a sort of lava dome, ready to erupt with the smallest fissure. While every transgression does not need a coach's attention, having a pressure-relief point short of an eruption is a good plan. If you develop your player leadership, interventions are less likely. The other side of the coin is having too many rules, and as previously mentioned, the better way is Urban Meyer's player self-policing through "above the line and below the line" standards.

I witnessed numerous occasions where the team leaders demonstrated uncanny abilities to push the team to a new level of performance, or a personal record (PR). Whether it was a bench-press weight, wall-squat time, or the daily competition, the leaders pushed and encouraged the team. They set a great example to follow. Minnesota Gophers' football coach P. J. Fleck put it this way: "On bad teams, no one leads; on average teams, the coaches lead; but on elite teams, the players lead." The 2020 team certainly fell into the elite category, but fate and the virus had a different ending for the 2020 season. Regardless, the 2020 team has the elusive elite team traits of trust and caring and that is a definition of success.

Elite players realize what each player's purpose is. A good, elite player's impact can be described with the difference between blowing out a birthday candle and a California wildfire. To blow out a single birthday candle, it takes air crossing the flame at about twenty mph. If you have a brush fire going, wind blowing across the flames at twenty mph literally turns a small flame into a conflagration. Developing elite players creates a team wildfire, which spreads throughout a team.

It was exciting to be a part of the process of watching our 2020 players develop and coalesce into a team. I cannot think of a more satisfying feeling than watching grown men discover the powerful effect of working as a unit. The synergy working as a unit creates is a fundamental lesson I have kept since my days at the Air Force Academy. The inescapable truth is that my life has been lived best when belonging to a team, a unit, or a crew.

I wrote previously about Air Force Academy training and what it instilled in me. The most fundamental lessons revolved around "we before me," the goal of the team, the mission, and the purpose. I mentioned S.E.R.E. training and the POW camp experience. One of the first things the POW guards did was separate us into individuals and eliminate the chance of establishing mutual support.

Another teaching point was the creation of loyalty to your squadron through squadron logos and mascots. Being a "Tiger," part of "Thirsty Third," "Fighting Fourth," or "Orcas" helped me build an identity. Team cohesion and purpose grows when people have an identity, something that binds them together, changes the "me to we," and gives them a purpose beyond themselves.

The coaching process includes so many elements, but creating a team personality, a positive culture, is the bedrock to success. Another key is learning how to deal with failure and how to recover from failure. Baseball is a humbling teacher. Batters who hit successfully three out of ten times throughout their career are hall of fame material. Three of ten is a .300 batting average, and it means they failed to get a hit 70 percent of the time. Think of that statement. Can you imagine a chief executive officer of any company claiming success is doing well 30 percent of the time? How long would that CEO last? I would venture, not long. No matter your failure rate, each failure should be kindling for the continuous-improvement fire. The only permanent failure is giving up.

The discipline, self-image, ego, and mental gymnastics needed to overcome a 70 percent failure rate would cause most to shy away from attempting to play at all. Overcoming a fear of failure is one of the first lessons that baseball teaches its participants. If you do not have a technique or strategy to overcome failure or adversity, you will not play baseball for long. An analogy would be an art student facing a blank canvas. If the student never lays a brush to canvas, she will never fail, but with each stroke and each new canvas, the past lessons contribute to the future masterpiece. Both coach and art teacher need special motivational tools to deal with that fear of failure. You have successes, and you have opportunities to learn. If you choose to dwell on the failure and not the learning process toward success, you are stuck and cannot move further toward success. Stephen Covey defined that reaction this way: "It is response-ability rather than responsibility." How we react to failure, what lesson we learn, can be the factor in how we respond to the next challenge we face. No matter how hard you practice, condition, or play, you will fail. Jon Leister, pitcher for the Chicago Cubs, described it this way:

> "I will probably start thirty games in a season, assuming I stay healthy. Of those thirty games, in five of them, I will absolutely be lights out, unhittable. Five of the games, I will be terrible. Of the remaining twenty games, what I do, how I adjust because I don't have my best stuff, determines whether I have an MVP season or a terrible season."

What this means is he will have some terrible pitching innings, innings where he will play and fail, but how he deals with those innings, how he adjusts to the failures, and what he learns is working and not working makes all the difference. How does he get to what's important next?

Folks who are fixer-uppers or tinkerers know that the key to handling any situation is having a full toolbox. Whether its needle-nosed pliers or a power saw or a cordless drill, certain tools prove essential for any job that needs to be completed. And it is the same with coaching! We need to have a stocked toolbox, so we are able to deal with the disgruntled player, the starter whose spot is about to be taken, as well as the athletic director that wants you to fundraise a seemingly impossible amount of money each year. The difference is just "that much." The tools are there; we just may be out of practice.

Team development is an ongoing lesson, and I want to pass on lessons before others experience these lessons as I did, learning the hard way. Teaching fundamentals, practicing advanced skills, and fine-tuning plays are all irreplaceable tasks. Remember, I want to be like a coffee bean, turning water into something that smells good, tastes good, and positively changes simple water as you grind it, brew it, and pour it. Just like coffee, coaching is a process where you introduce, grind, brew, and pour yourself into the team to transform them into gourmet coffee.

Good coaches will always pursue relentless execution of fundamentals. But elite, high-performing teams relentlessly build culture and trust and clearly define roles and expectations. Just like good basketball teams have good ball-passers who share in the scoring, my resolve is to be a good information-passer with the goal of making a difference. If I can pass on some of what I've learned, then I have answered the question of *why* I coach. Not in a "my way" format, but in a way that presents the information as *This worked for me, try it or don't*. We can learn together.

15 – THAT'S THE DIFFERENCE

> "When you can do the common things in life
> in an uncommon way, you will command
> the attention of the world."
> —George Washington Carver

The coach of a major university baseball team—we will call him Tim—tells a story about when he played Division I baseball. As a freshman riding the bench, he remembers observing a teammate stretch a single into a double. The teammate was actually Tim's unofficial "big brother." Standing at second base, "big brother" motioned into the dugout, holding his thumb and index finger about an inch apart, to which Tim signaled back in like manner, not knowing exactly the message. Later, as Tim's team built a sizable lead, Tim was sent in as a third-base replacement.

As is always the case in baseball, the newest substitute immediately gets a ball hit to him, as if to baptize substitute players as soon as possible. And sure enough, Tim caught a hard-hit ground ball with his backhand and made a throw to his "big brother" at first base in the nick of time for the out. His "big brother" immediately motioned to Tim, holding his thumb and index finger about an inch apart, with Tim motioning back likewise. Sides retired, Tim hustled into the dugout, and he asked his "big brother" what the thumb and index finger sign meant. The answer, in classic baseball vernacular, was that the signal indicated the "difference" between a good hit, a good play, and success. The "big brother" said, "That's the difference. It's not much, but that's the difference between elite and average."

The process of making "that difference" certainly fits the previously mentioned Carol Dweck growth-mindset model as opposed to the fixed-mindset model. Those who embrace growth are apparent. They are the people who continuously seek new opportunities and potential areas for growth. The "fixed mindset" looks at success as a destination, and says things like, "I will be happy/content if only_____ happens (fill in the blank)." People who look at success as a process realize that happiness and contentment come from embracing the process. Athletes who run one more lap than required embrace the idea that one more repetition epitomizes growth. My goal is to instill a growth mindset and help an athlete or business-person to make that little difference in their performance.

One practical illustration of how a growth mindset works is in a story about retired Admiral James Stockdale. Shot down while flying over North Vietnam during the Vietnam War, Admiral Stockdale was captured and spent nearly eight years in the infamous "Hanoi Hilton" as a prisoner of war. Years later in an interview, Admiral Stockdale was asked how he managed to survive so many years when many of the other aviators captured after him did not. His answer was that he accepted his condition, while those who did not survive held out finite hopes, such as "If we can just wait until Christmas, we will all be released," and when Christmas came with no release, the timeline changed to, "if we can just maintain until Easter." When Easter arrived, again, there was no release. These POWs lost hope and found despair and finally death as they gave up. Meanwhile, Admiral Stockdale and a few other survivors real-ized the importance of living one day at a time, celebrating each day's minor victories.

The same phenomenon occurs with first-time marathoners. Statistics show that half to three-quarters of these first-time runners do not finish, and the most remarkable thing is that the majority of the athletes drop out at about the twenty-mile mark (of a 26.2-mile race). So close to the end! There are a variety of reasons, but the one of the most recurring is mental fatigue. Those who do finish, for the most part, do so by maintaining the thought of completing one mile at a time, as in "take care of this mile. Okay, that's done. Now take care of this mile."

"You gotta have heart" means providing the vision and the *why* a team does what it does. Sailors on old-time trading ships had a *why* for the trip. Maybe it was to bring spices, cotton, or any number of goods back to homeport. Paid by the trip, each sailor had defined roles, like setting sails, steering, and lookout. The daily routines could go on for months, but each sailor knew his role and knew why his job was important—where it fit in with the trading-goods business. Can you imagine the lack of purpose if the helmsman steered the ship wherever he wanted? Breaking down the required duties was seemingly unnecessary, and the inherent dangers were mere added motivators. Sailors did what they were supposed to do, because the *why* and purpose were clear.

We have a saying in my family. "Do what you're supposed to do and a little more, and then the rest of us have less to do and can do even more." One time, I pointed out to my wife that the line was kind of an oxymoron, to which she replied, tongue in cheek, "Don't call me names." The "do what you're supposed to do and a little more" logic is perfect and encourages initiative. I never understand how someone can sit back idly when there is work to be done. Jumping in to help should be part of your *why,* if you want to make a difference.

My long-range goal, the *why* I coach, is to make a difference by mentoring new leaders one person at a time. Potential leaders need to recognize the chasm between a subject-matter expert and a leader. A subject-matter expert does not automatically translate into being a good leader. The two positions have vastly different skill sets; however, a lot of the tools to be a leader are already in the new leader's toolbox; they just don't realize it, have never used the available tools, or were never really taught how to use the tools.

Subject-matter expertise is measured by projects, bottom lines, and hard data, while leadership skills are not easily measured and are sometimes referred to as "soft skills," because they are hard to quantify. You have to learn, regularly update, and exercise the skills of leadership. People make the assumption that moving into a leadership position is an easy transition, and that subject-matter expertise transfers easily. Instead, good leaders are developed, given chances to experience leading, and are lifelong learners. Some so-called experts brush off the development portion by claiming, "Oh, I had a management class in college. I am good to go" or "I supervise two other people in my office, and I've been doing this job for twenty years. I know how to lead." No. You are never completely done learning how to lead until the day you retire.

Leadership development must be an ongoing project in a team's process. Ongoing training and opportunities to learn leadership skills are indispensable. A team's leader or a company's leadership is the very foundation of any group or organization. Nurturing the roots of a fruit tree for harvesting the fruit is critical to team continuity and survival. Good and bad leadership skills make the difference between being a boss and being a leader. Bosses rely on authority, whereas leaders inspire teams to perform at levels they never thought possible. The guiding force behind successful teams and organizations is the leadership. Good leadership is "that difference" between elite and average performance.

Getting better every day must be integral to the process. Think of basketball's Michael Jordan, who after winning an NBA championship, would hold up one more finger than the total number of his championships, signifying that he and his teammates had already started working on the next championship. That is loving the process over the results.

Off-season is often spent in conditioning, but what about mental conditioning? The time used working on leadership and the mental approach is time well spent. I previously mentioned the importance of developing new leadership each year at the high-school and college level. Coaches can make a huge difference by empowering athletes through mental-approach training and taking them to a level of performance they never thought possible. The impact and influence of mental-approach coaching can help young athletes learn to overcome adversity, look at obstacles as opportunities, and gain comfort in uncomfortable situations. Experts say both forms of conditioning, physical and mental, need resistance training. I know I am a big resistance, physical-conditioning advocate; I resist most workouts by not even going.

Brian Cain, a mental performance coach, defines what he does as "the art and science of helping those you work with overcome mental barriers that trip them up and build the habits, behaviors, and routines they need to achieve their goals and perform at a high level—even when it's hard." Baseball coaches have all seen the MVP batting-cage player who cracks under pressure at the plate. Why are those batting-cage skills not transferable to actual game situations? Simple: Mental performance.

Some coaches claim that mental performance is innate and cannot be trained. I disagree. Just like leadership, mental-performance skills need to be planted, nurtured, and tended. These days, a typical high-school player can play a video game without fear of failure as he/she learns the basic game skills and strategies. A failure in a video game is met with a bit of disdain, a simple reset, and then back into the intensity of "leveling up" or winning a round with no thought of embarrassment or loss of face. Through trial and error, these teens learn to deal with failure and move on, recover, and refocus on the next trial. Why can't this release, recover, and refocus be taught to athletes? The athletes are simply playing another game. Why can't business leaders be taught the same thing? They are playing in a sort of competition, albeit with slightly different results.

In a different vein of thought, a positive leadership style motivates teams by utilizing a "we before me" mentality, where a team member is more concerned with letting the team down than they are of individual failure. Positive leadership is a continuous battle. It's not the Pollyanna high-school cheerleader "rah-rah." It is recognizing negativity, and knowing that succumbing to fear of the future contributes nothing to W.I.N. (what's important next). In baseball, it's striking out and analyzing what pitches you saw, so you're ready for the next at bat. In football, it is falling behind twenty to zero in the first half and making adjustments at halftime. In business, it's the understanding that you have no control over a late shipment and coming up with another option. Positive leadership is never giving up on finding a solution. It's embracing the grind.

Coaches need to spend time on focus, motivation, recovery, routines, imagery, and breathing. Think of elite Olympians before a performance or competition. Those competitors have preparation, diet, pre-competition routines, in-competition affirmations, and post-competition routines. Do you remember watching Michael Phelps, Olympic gold-medalist swimmer, listening to music through headphones while moving his hands, imagining his swimming motions and picturing success? Or did you see Picabo Street, Olympic slalom skier, standing in a waiting room with her eyes closed as she moved her body and visualized herself skiing through the slalom gates? In short, mental performance should not be shortchanged and can make "the difference."

16 – TAKEAWAYS

"Life is all about takeaways from great people
and giveaways to the needy ones."
—Vikrmn

The usual advice writers receive when penning a self-help, personal, and/or professional-development book is to begin with the end in mind. I waited until I was almost halfway finished, because that is how my writing process seemed to work best. I get ideas, and I just start writing them down. Then, an epiphany occurs, and I try to tie them all together. I watched a beautiful process in action where one writer took to writing different ideas all over a scratch piece of paper, circling each like a cartoon speech bubble. Then he connected the bubbles with lines that made sense to him.

Do you remember going bowling for the first time when you were a kid? The balls were heavy and the bumpers were raised to keep your ball in the lane, heading toward the ten pins. With the bumpers so high, the only way to miss the pins was if you didn't have enough forward momentum on the ball, or if the ball bounced over the sides! Just like in bowling, as long as you are strong enough to propel your thoughts, even though your writing may bounce from side-to-side, eventually, you will hit some pins and score. As you learn and strengthen your skill, you will, in time, bowl down the middle of the lane and gradually improve your score. And you will have no need for bumpers.

The point of the bowling analogy is to encourage someone to begin writing. If you don't ever roll the ball, in the bumper analogy, you will never knock any pins down. There are a thousand ways of writing—some better than others—but there are only three or four wrong ways leading your writing to nowhere. Robyn Ramirez, a producer, beckons us to take "massive imperfect action," and Nike's "Just Do It" slogan comes to mind as well. "Massive imperfect action" means jumping in feet first and embracing the process, the struggle. Failure is the first step toward success, unless you let failure define your writing. So, if you feel you need to tell your story, do it; reveal your vulnerability. Yes, if this book becomes popular, I will forever be known as the guy who survived a heart attack and wrote a book, but if I connected with someone besides myself and made a difference, it was worth it. One meme making the rounds says, "Be Bold, Be Brave, Begin." I like that.

My point is that this book became very personal to me, and I was urged by my wife to get comfortable with being uncomfortable. "Start writing and keep writing" was her mantra to me. My career-changing event occurred over twelve years ago, and thinking about that event, taking this manuscript off the top shelf of my bookcase every day, was both cathartic and gut wrenching. Brené Brown tells us that, to build a relationship, we must reveal our vulnerability and earn the trust of those around us. Twelve years to confront my heart attack is a long time to carry such a heavy load, or baggage. Eventually, the time came to expose the vulnerability, despite the knuckle-dragging Neanderthal in me—the man who used to say, "I got this, and I don't do emotions." Hmmm, is it bad to have a *Y* chromosome? That is a question for another time.

So here come the takeaways.

- **Life is a series of events.** Some look at them as challenges, while others see opportunities. My heart attack started as a challenge, but with the help of friends and relatives, the event morphed into an opportunity. I had to find something I loved to do so "I would never work a day in my life again." My best friend would say I never worked a day in my life anyway.

- **E+P=O:** Events plus our positive response equals the outcome. Events are uncontrollable. There will be an outcome, and the best we can do is influence the outcome through our actions. Be the positive response and control the controllables.

- **Popular lore claims you are the sum of the five people you are around the most, family excepted.** Find the ones who care, can reveal their deepest secrets, or communicate their vulnerabilities. These are the ones who are committed and care for you. Those five make you better. A team environment, which creates psychologically safe relations, is the key to high-performing teams. Remember the Google Aristotle[2] experiment, where the talented team finished behind the team who develop an environment where everyone felt safe expressing ideas, able to easily "brainstorm" without fear or embarrassment? Find that.

Here is an interesting aspect to the people you learn from and who challenge and support you: Redwoods are the tallest trees in the world. One could stand at the base of a redwood in awe as the top disappears into the clouds. Interestingly though, redwoods have one of the shallowest root systems, which only go underground a few feet. The reason they stay rooted and don't topple in high winds or in heavy rains is the same reason

---

2   Michael Schneider, "Google Spent 2 Years Studying 180 Teams. The Most Successful Ones Shared These 5 Traits" 19 July 2017, Inc. magazine. https://www.inc.com/michael-schneider/google-thought-they-knew-how-to-create-the-perfect.html

you stay rooted and don't topple under duress. The redwoods' roots are intertwined for support. You, too, need to intertwine with your friends for support. If a redwood's success is measured by its height, and its health is based on its root system, the other redwoods are its support system.

We get all kinds of examples of support from those around us, especially the five people we are around the most. If you are not seeing examples or getting support from those five, maybe it is time for some different friends or acquaintances. Satisfaction comes from changing our challenges into opportunities, and we get encouragement from the five people who influence us the most.

- I find that living and enjoying the moment is a good philosophy. Past mistakes and success really have no bearing on the present, except for the lessons they teach. Like baseball, the past is in the scorebook, and we cannot change it. What we can do is go back to the statistics to see trends or review the lessons we learned. Once we have the lesson, though, we must drop the regret. It's the same story for the future. We have no control over the future, so instead of fearing the future, have hope. As previously stated, if the future has not happened, why would we pick fear over hope? Hope tendered while acknowledging the controllables versus uncontrollables lights the path toward your goal.

- Author Jon Gordon tells us, "We don't get burned out because of what we do; we get burned out because we forget *why* we do it (emphasis mine)." If you are constantly looking at the scorebook and focusing on the results, you are not growing or improving. You are forgetting the lesson. Results are history. Be forward-looking and remember *why* you are working on a goal. Concentrate on the process, what's important next, or what's important now using the W.I.N. acronym as a reminder.

I lost my *why* for a good while. I was impatient for results. I was impatient for the return to the job I loved but would never have again. I found that a career "do-over" takes time, and there are no steps to skip, no shortcuts. The process requires perseverance, and while you may get advice and encouragement, it boils down to a change that happens in your heart. God has a plan, and bullheaded people like me are not always receptive—at least not quickly.

My change took twelve years. It took that long to realize that I am exactly where I am supposed to be. Teacher, coach, speaker, father, husband, and soon-to-be grandfather. I am comfortable in the uncomfortable role of my one word: MENTOR. Mentoring means helping others, volunteering service, guiding others to embrace opportunities, and teaching others to be comfortable in uncomfortable situations. If you do not feel you can affect others, think of the Dalai Lama's quote, "If you think you are too small to make a difference, try sleeping with a mosquito."

New York Times bestselling author Mark Batterson urges us to stop living like the purpose in life is to arrive safely at death. His book *In the Pit with a Lion on a Snowy Day* is based on a Bible story from 2 Samuel 23. The book tells the true story of an ancient warrior named Benaiah who chased a lion into a pit on a snowy day and then killed it. For most people, that situation wouldn't just be a problem; it would be the last problem they ever faced. For Benaiah, it was an opportunity to step into his destiny. After defeating the lion, he landed his dream job as King David's bodyguard and eventually became commander-in-chief of Israel's army under King Solomon.

Help yourself first, and learn from failure. Go out and develop a new skill, practice until you cannot get it wrong, and then practice to do it faster. Go fight the lion. Go face adversity and stretch your comfort zone. This is the very basis of the continuous-improvement process.

- The difference between ordinary and exceptional, of average versus elite, is that little difference. Those people, teams, and organizations that thrive are the ones that embrace change and growth. You can see it in innovative companies like Apple. The team at Apple started with the innovative idea of desktop computers for everyone, then moved to laptops, then iPods, then iPads, then iWatches, then downloading music, and now into areas never dreamed of before, such as automated driving cars and drone delivery. Apple isn't still stuck building desktops, but rather boldly entering new, unexplored markets. Again, "Be bold, be brave, and begin."

Those who do not adapt to the realities, those who throw their hands up in defeat, and those who are comfortable in their circumstances fail to move to the next level or make much difference. This is the fixed-mindset crowd. You have to admire the innovators who never stop learning or growing. The innovators like my brother-in-law, adapting his violin classes to online, or the hairdresser doing virtual haircuts. Those are the people who inspire and who make that little difference, which in turn, makes the world a better place, one person at a time.

"Each of you should use whatever gift you have received to serve others, as faithful stewards of God's grace in various forms." (1 Peter 4:10, NIV)

If you want to change challenges into opportunities, it *Takes More Than Heart.*

ABOUT THE AUTHOR

Dennis Mellen, a USAF Academy graduate (1975), is a retired Air Force pilot after serving as a lieutenant colonel and chief pilot for 20 years until his retirement from the Air Force Reserves in 1996. At the time, he simultaneously worked as an instructor pilot and fleet captain at Alaska Airlines where he was the head of training over 550 pilots and 40 instructors. He was also part of the instructor cadre instrumental in establishing the Alaska Airlines route structure in eastern Russia from the destinations: Vladivostok, Khabarovsk, Magadan, and Petropavlovsk-Kamchatskiy. And as a veteran, he participated in the Desert One preparation, he was deployed to Sudan (in 1986) to counter Libyan incursions in Chad, and participated in Desert Shield/Storm. After retiring in 2012 from his 28-year flying career due to a heart attack, Dennis continued searching for a new purpose and new opportunities. He worked in aviation management at two air carriers heading up their training and standardization departments. He also worked as a training consultant and certified International Air Transport Association Operation Safety auditor before becoming a high school baseball coach, speaker, and author. His goal with his first book is to provide motivation, education, and humor to inspire those who face serious challenges in their lives. Dennis and his wife, Heidi of 37 years, live in the Chicago suburbs, and they have four sons and just welcomed their first grandchild as of August 2020—they look forward to helping raise their granddaughter, as well as welcoming more grandchildren.

 # BE A BEAN

How could you add to your continuous improvement and take your team to the next performance level?

A leader is the biggest influence on team culture.

Be A Bean, Be A Transformer.
Change your team from ordinary water
into gourmet coffee.

For Power of Positive Leadership
Presentation/Workshop (live or virtual) opportunities go to:
https://www.beabean.net

CPSIA information can be obtained
at www.ICGtesting.com
Printed in the USA
LVHW052319220421
685283LV00007B/313